AN ENGLISH EDUCATION
A Perspective of Eton

AN ENGLISH EDUCATION

A Perspective of Eton

RICHARD OLLARD

COLLINS
14 St. James's Place, London
1982

William Collins Sons & Co Ltd
London · Glasgow · Sydney · Auckland
Toronto · Johannesburg

British Library CIP data

Ollard, Richard
    An English education: a perspective of Eton.
    1. Eton College
    I. Title
373.422'96   LF795.E84

First published 1982
© Richard Ollard 1982
ISBN 0 00 216495 7
Composition in Garamond by Filmtype Services Limited, Scarborough, North Yorkshire
Made and Printed in Great Britain by
William Collins Sons & Co Ltd Glasgow

To
GRIZEL HARTLEY
who loved Eton
and shewed so many masters and boys
what there was to love in it

CONTENTS

PREFACE
AND ACKNOWLEDGMENTS

An author who explains what his book is about and how he came to write it may be thought to apologise too much. But there are so many books about Eton that some elucidation of what this one purports to contain may be useful.

One of my colleagues in Collins observed to me that there had been no book about Eton between the two World Wars. I had known the place at first hand at the end of that period and from reading and conversation had some impression of the two preceding decades. Having written chiefly about seventeenth century people where documents and portraits offer the biographer his only material I thought it would be interesting to work from the life. I volunteered and was accepted.

Institutions, like people, embody their own past. One cannot write, at least I cannot write, about a person or a situation without first doing my best to understand how they came to be such as they are. The past and the present are part of each other. I have therefore tried to isolate those elements which seem to me to have been of persistent and characteristic importance in the long and fascinating history of the school, the better to throw the focus where it should fall in the period with which I am specifically concerned.

To define by negatives, this book has nothing to say about Eton as it has developed since the Second War, except very occasionally by extension or implication. It is not about games. There are no esoteric jokes. Where I have found it necessary to use Etonian terminology I have explained it, re-inforcing this with a brief glossary.

My debts to other books have all, I hope, been acknowledged either in the references or in the brief bibliography. For permission to use manuscript material listed in the bibliography I wish to express my thanks to Lady Home of the Hirsel, B.J.W. Hill, Esq., Edward Hodgkin, Esq., the Provost and Fellows of Eton College and the Master and Fellows of Magdalene College, Cambridge. My debts to old and new friends who have so generously contributed ideas and recollections are not so easily listed. Indeed if I were to attempt a comprehensive statement of them I should try the reader's patience. At Eton the hospitality of Giles St Aubyn and of Michael Meredith, most helpful of archivists, have made every visit a pleasure. To those who taught me as a boy and have further enlightened my understanding in this connexion I am particularly grateful to Richard Martineau, Francis Cruso, Oliver Van Oss and above all Walter Hamilton who crowned his many kindnesses by reading my manuscript, saving me from many errors and drawing my attention to much that I had missed. Among my seniors who have generously allowed me to come and talk to them I am particularly grateful to the present Provost of Eton, Lord Charteris of Amisfield, Sir Harold Acton, the Hon. David Astor, Sir Robert Birley, Sir Rupert Hart-Davis, Mr Felix Markham and Sir Roger Mynors. John Grigg, Oliver Knox and Kenneth Rose have allowed old friendship to be put to the proof of reading my manuscript. Their comments and suggestions have, as so often in the past forty years or so, cleared my mind, raised my spirits and improved my expression. My brother Peter who was elected to a scholarship eight years earlier than I has discharged the same kind office to my great benefit.

My greatest debt is to Peter Lawrence whose knowledge of and feeling for the unobvious aspects of Eton in the twentieth century is rivalled only by his generosity in putting it at the disposal of those who are less well equipped. For answering innumerable questions, for lending me a complete set of *Etoniana*, that invaluable publication which he has himself so well anthologised in *The Encouragement of Learning* (Wilton,

1980), and finally for reading my manuscript I wish to record my gratitude to him.

None of my benefactors here mentioned are in any way responsible for such errors of fact, taste and opinion as have survived their scrutiny. An author must claim credit for something.

—————————⁓—————————

CHAPTER ONE

The Idea of Eton

THERE IS NO UNDERSTANDING ENGLAND of the twenties and thirties without understanding Eton. During the past hundred and fifty years it has played no small part in forming the mind and temper, the character and taste of the country. In the first half of the twentieth century it would be hard to think of any comparable influence exerted by any institution or even by any self-constituted group. The number of Old Etonians in modern Cabinets has been often remarked, not always approvingly. The representation of this pious and learned foundation in the boardrooms of the City and in the direction of great industrial and commercial enterprise is a commonplace of political controversy. What is not so often remembered is Eton's contribution to the life of the mind and to the world of letters. George Orwell and Cyril Connolly, J.B.S. Haldane and Maynard Keynes, Aldous Huxley and Reynolds Stone, are enough to remind the reader that it was considerable. Even the fashionable treachery of the age had a conspicuous exemplar in Guy Burgess.

Much of this might be explained on obvious grounds. Eton during this period was rich, famous and aristocratic. Those who could be so characterised or were ambitious of such a description sent their sons there. Born to wealth and place no wonder that Etonians should ascend by the easy gradations of snobbery and nepotism to preferment in Tory politics and well-paid jobs in the City. One might as well exclaim at so many of them becoming Masters of Fox Hounds. As to Orwell and the others they were the fortunate beneficiaries of an exceptionally liberal

scholarship endowment that by virtue of its generosity attracted
a strong field of competitors, themselves enjoying in their turn
certain essential advantages, such as the opportunity of learning
Greek and Latin, denied to the poor. The Old Etonians came
out on top because thanks to the prevailing social system they
had started there.

The very sound of the name Eton lends colour to this view.
Like that other glutinous dissyllable 'élite' its subliminal suggestion of sleekness and success elicits among Englishmen and
others familiar with things English a resentment that is not
provoked by the mention of Winchester or Rugby, of
Wellington or Marlborough. If these were the names of characters in a Restoration comedy and not of great public schools we
should know at once that the last four were plain, bluff, old-
fashioned country gentlemen, a little coarse, perhaps, but essentially good-hearted, while Eton would be the man of fashion,
selfish, cynical and predatory. In the period treated in this book
the school dress, tail-coats, top hats, or, for the smaller boys,
Eton jackets topped by the starched slopes of an Eton collar,
seemed an ostentatious and arrogant defiance of contemporary
society. To those who had suffered the futilities and frustrations
of the old boy network it was hardly necessary to look further
for its complete embodiment.

Whether such instinctive perceptions are true or false they
identify Eton as the type, the image, the expression of forces
and tendencies diffused throughout the nation. Granted the
existence of an old boy network with all its ramifications of
clannishness and cliquery it surely needs to be spread far wider
if it is to be effective. Harrow and Charterhouse and Westminster and many more will claim their share. What, apart from
superficialities, is so special to Eton? How and when did it come
to be thought so outstanding? Whatever it was or was not in the
twenties and thirties it was not a new creation. The fact of
continuity, fascinating in itself, presents a puzzle like that of the
tortoise and the hare. We know perfectly well that the Eton so
lovingly evoked in late Victorian memoirs is not, except in the
most limited topographical sense, the same place as the bear-
garden of a hundred years earlier. Yet instinct, feeling, usage

combine to submerge this recognition, truism that it is of all our ancient institutions, Parliament, the Monarchy, the Church, the Law, the Navy. Change is the law of life. But in England it is a law submitted to without enthusiasm, obeyed in the letter rather than in the spirit. We keep, if we can, the outward forms when we redesign the machinery.

This historical trait is as conspicuous in the universities of Oxford and Cambridge as in the great schools from which they have drawn, and still draw, so many of their members. The porter's lodge, the hall, the chapel, the buttery, the terms and the things, are still serving the purposes for which they were designed in the middle ages. If William of Wykeham were to step through the front gate of New College, if Archbishop Laud were to revisit his quadrangle at St John's, both men would surely swell with pride and pleasure at the loving care with which their splendid benefactions were maintained. But can we be so confident of their continued approval if the curricular and extra-curricular activities of the dons and undergraduates were explained to them? The continuity of institutions like the longevity of individuals is one of the strongest if least palpable bonds that hold society together. Rooted in sentiment, hostile to rational analysis, it draws to co-operation individuals and tendencies that might otherwise find themselves at odds. It also draws them to combine in obstructing innovation and in preserving the privileges of exclusiveness. In nature, or out of it, there is no good thing that cannot be put to a bad use. Bacteria are axiomatically the friend of man, even though there are many contexts in which they are his enemy. A sterilised world would not support life. A society that had purged itself of all bodies with some degree of organic continuity is unimaginable.

But what, in the case of Eton, is the animating principle? What gives it its life? What distinguishes its flavour? As with the ancient universities the most widely accepted answer must be the place itself, the beauty of its setting, the nobility and individuality of the buildings that embody the original foundation. The chapel and Lupton's Tower, the School Yard of which they form part, the cloisters and the playing fields, long but now no more elm-shaded, bordering the river: with what a summer afternoon laziness the mind slips into this elegiac identification. From the verse of Winthrop Mackworth Praed and William Johnson Cory to the prose of uncounted memoirs and autobiographies how often it has been evoked. Powerful or merely mawkish, such expression of the image of Eton certainly affects the actuality. It is impossible to think of the people that we know well without interpreting their character, their emotions, their thoughts, through their physical presence: tones of voice, expressions of feature, ways of moving or staying still. We all know the shock of recognition, the sudden enlightenment, of meeting someone in the flesh with whom we have long been familiar from reading or from correspondence. The physical contact extends and clarifies our perception, makes it real as opposed to theoretical. It colours and dominates our whole idea so that we come, naturally, to fuse the material person with the abstract personality already perceived before any meeting took place.

The intimates of Eton can read in its fabric and its landscape what they have found there. If they have themselves been at school there it will be surprising if their vision is not touched even if at some remove by the rarely placid experience of growing up. Whether the tone be that of the blandest and rosiest or of Captain Grimes's robust vindication of the public school system: 'It made life hell at a time when life was bound to be hell anyway', the cool and the equable are scarcely to be looked for. The beauty of the place and the turbulence of adolescents living cheek by jowl are constant if sometimes disguised elements in every recollection of Eton.

A long history does not necessarily engender a lively sense of the past. Most Americans know much more about the history of their country than most Englishmen know of theirs. The Eton of the nineteen twenties and thirties prided itself on its antiquity but knew in general very little about it. Some of the masters and some old boys were distinguished antiquaries and published during this period a wealth of original material relating to the history of the school. But the size and variety and success of the place relegated such studies to the sidelines. The idea that it came from everlasting and would go to everlasting was strong. It was assumed that nothing would change very much during the process: it was similarly assumed that nothing had changed very much in the past, or that if it had it was in so far distant a past, the past of monks and nuns and knights in armour, as to belong to legend rather than to history. Eton, so the received idea went, had escaped the high seriousness of Dr Arnold and the tiresome priggery of his reforms. We could listen to Lytton Strachey sniggering over his death-bed (surely one of the most vulgar passages in English prose) and congratulate ourselves on our uninterrupted descent from the eighteenth century. The classical education, that is the teaching of Greek and Latin, was still the staple of our system. We were, to be sure, taught French and mathematics and the sciences and divinity and history. After taking School Certificate (the great public examination of the period) we were free to drop the classics altogether and specialise in something else. But the tone of the school was still predominantly classical. The subject enjoyed the kind of pre-eminence that during the same decades gunnery did in the Royal Navy. In both cases a long tradition was nearing its end, but there were no symptons of senility. The classics at Eton were self-confident, vigorous and fresh, attracting, in spite of the parade-ground discipline of scholarship, some whose tastes lay elsewhere. I need hardly add that the classics are still taught at Eton, with the same verve and brilliance as before. What has ended is not the subject but its paramountcy.

The distant prospect of Eton College conceals discrepancies and discontinuities that become clear on a closer view. Some account of its history is essential to any understanding of what it was at any particular point. The classical education, for instance, that set the intellectual and aesthetic tone of the period between the wars was by no means the same in content, in technique and in range as that offered in the eighteenth century. The ethos of the school, the limits of tolerable behaviour, the ideas of what was to be admired, changed and no doubt still change, sometimes radically, sometimes gradually. In its external relations Eton certainly did not always enjoy the standing in the life of the nation that it did in the twenties and thirties.

In its internal constitution, its economy, its class structure it has changed at least as much as the country itself but not necessarily in the same way or at the same time. As a historical phenomenon it can only be understood in historical terms.

The first, most conspicuous characteristic of the foundation is that it was royal and that it was rich. No other great school can claim so persistent and so intimate a connexion with the monarchy. This has not been an unmixed blessing. That Eton and King's were the favourite project of King Henry VI natur- ally exposed them to the greatest risk when the fortunes of war went against him. That he had endowed them so splendidly made them glitter in the eyes of the nobles and churchmen who had backed the winning side. Eton lost much: but it was thanks to the favour of the new King, Edward IV, or as some say to that of his mistress, that so much was retained. Henry VI's choice of site meant that the place was never out of the royal eye. As it grew richer the elections to fellowships and to the post of Provost became important pieces of patronage, too valuable to escape the notice of courtiers and of governments. The College beer had such a reputation that Charles II often had it sent up when the court was at Windsor: indeed his father had been supplied with it in the melancholy days of his imprisonment in the castle immediately before his trial and execution. Queen Elizabeth, herself perhaps the most highly educated of all our sovereigns, often visited the place. Even her terrifying father signalised his approval by granting it together with Winchester and the universities of Oxford and Cambridge a special exemp- tion from ecclesiastical taxation.[1] But it was George III who adopted the school into his particular and personal affections. No Old Etonian, scarcely any boy in the school, could have taken a more anxious interest in the tremendous trifles of school life. If none of his successors have identified themselves quite so whole-heartedly with their schoolboy neighbours, all have shown a more than formal benevolence.

The riches with which Eton was endowed and which have been added to it have also had their disadvantages. The

1 27 Henry VIII c. 42.

disciplined, quasi-monastic life that the Founder had envisaged for the recipients of his bounty softened into the comfortable independence of the seventeenth century, degenerating into the fat complacency of the eighteenth and ending in the hysterical shrieks of enraged selfishness before the measured tread and unanswerable questions of the Victorian reformers. The clerical resident Fellows of Eton perished unlamented. Their luxury was indecent whilst the scholars were so inadequately fed and so meanly lodged that by the nineteenth century College, the institution founded for them, was often only half full. Easy money exerts too powerful a magnetic field. Institutions, principles, aspirations are sensitive to its pull. Would the Founder, had he been enabled to foresee the first five centuries of Eton's history, have set more careful limits to the use of his gifts? Such as he did set were largely evaded or defied. Royalty and riches can turn the soberest head: from the first they have lain at the heart of Eton. It is one of the paradoxes of the place that they were put there by one of the most unworldly, unroyal of English kings.[2]

What did Henry VI intend in founding Eton? First, and overwhelmingly, he intended an act of simple piety and adoration, having specially in mind the exaltation of the Virgin Mary. On the original seal of the College, she appears as the central dominant figure with the King kneeling to the right of a shield bearing the College arms on which she is standing. The lilies on that shield were originally intended as her own heraldic symbols and only later re-styled in the grant of arms as 'the brightest flowers redolent of every kind of knowledge'. The original constitution of the College provided for a Provost, ten fellows, four clerks, six choristers, a schoolmaster, twenty-five poor scholars and twenty-five poor and infirm men. The thrust was clearly devotional and charitable, with a strong secondary impulse toward education.

In the course of a few years this was modified. The almshouse element was scrapped. Worship and its expression in building

---

2 His latest biographer criticizes the evidence for his personal holiness with learning and wit. See Bertram Wolffe *Henry VI* (1981), especially the first and last chapters.

defined themselves as the leading idea. The present chapel is only the choir of the church the Founder had in mind when he laid the first stone in 1441. Had his plans been carried out there would only have been a handful of cathedrals in England to rival its size. But on the educational side the Founder's conception emerged as ever more markedly imitative of that of William of Wykeham. Sixty years earlier Wykeham had eclipsed all previous benefactions to learning by his double foundation of Winchester and New College, Oxford. Winchester was to be the grammar school for New College which was strictly forbidden to admit undergraduates from any other source. Two years after admission a Fellowship at New College followed automatically. Unless he inherited money and thus no longer satisfied the statutory requirement of poverty the Fellow could continue in residence until he took a benefice or entered a monastic order. Universities in the middle ages were of course exclusively clerical. This was the model that Henry VI took, matching Winchester with Eton and New College with King's. The same limitations and exclusions were exactly reproduced. King's could only fill its vacancies from Eton. Every year about the end of July the Provost of King's accompanied by two of his Fellows rode over from Cambridge to make the election. At the same time the Eton authorities elected scholars to replace those who were going to King's or being superannuated.

The Wykehamist character of Henry VI's foundation can hardly be exaggerated. Not only did the King pay several visits to Winchester while he was planning his school, not only did he copy many of Wykeham's statutes word for word: he manned his new venture with the products of these institutions. The marriage of these minds, Wykeham one of the most capable and thorough administrators in our history, and Henry VI who proved himself to be unfitted for any kind of executive authority, is one of the strangest elements in the Eton pedigree. It may be remote but importance is not always a matter of proximity.

For the first four centuries of their lives Eton and its sister foundation at Cambridge saw a great deal too much of each other and too little of anyone else. The powerful statutory defences that William of Wykeham had constructed against the

external enemies of the fourteenth century obstructed movement and development in succeeding generations. The fidelity
with which they had been imitated at Eton and King's produced
the same effects. Not until the Victorian Commissions brought
the full artillery of legislation to bear on these venerable fortif-
ications were their cramping, confining tendencies at last
eliminated. The worst effects were felt at King's. The intellectual inbreeding of a college that could not cross-fertilise itself
from the rest of the university can be easily imagined. The place
became a kind of club to which the fortunate members were
elected for life, excused from duties and comfortably accommodated. The condition of Eton never sank to this torpor
though it was coloured by it. The Provost and Fellows were by
statute required to be members of this insulated corporation
and the scholars were its apprentices. But the Head Master and
his assistants were not, though from Queen Elizabeth's
accession there were only four Head Masters in the succeeding
three centuries (not counting the irregularities of the Civil War
and Interregnum) who were not the products of Eton and
King's. The position of the assistant masters had customarily
become a jealously guarded preserve of the system. It was Dr
Keate who early in the nineteenth century appointed the first
assistant not to be a Fellow of King's, though the man half
satisfied convention by having been a scholar of Eton. Twenty
years later Dr Goodford became the first Head Master to ap-
point to his staff one who had not even this fig-leaf with which
to cover his nakedness. The newcomer was none the less an
Etonian who himself became one of the greatest Head Masters,
Dr Warre. But he was an Oppidan, not a Colleger.

This, the single salient class distinction of Eton in every age,
requires some elucidation. Oppidans were originally so called
because they lodged in the town (*oppidum*) as opposed to the
College inhabited by the scholars. Yet the earliest name under
which their position is regulated in the statutes is that of Commensals, clearly showing, as indeed the statutes go on to specify,
that they shall share the common meal in hall that is the heart
of the collegiate system. Even the Commensals are divided into
two classes: twenty of noble birth who are to sit at the higher

tables in hall like the Gentleman or Nobleman Commoners of the universities, and an unspecified number who are to sit with the Collegers. The education provided is free but otherwise, unlike the seventy scholars, they are to pay their way. Apart from the twenty grandees, the earliest Collegers and the earliest Oppidans appear to have come from much the same section of society. Serfs were not eligible. If the scholars were by definition poorer than the Oppidans they manifestly enjoyed a superior status: they were there by right, the others by courtesy; and from the term Commensal and from the size of the hall it would seem that they were expected to outnumber the Oppidans.

Writers on Eton between the wars have either emphatically or implicitly pointed out the great difference between the two categories. At an earlier period things went far beyond sneering and snobbery: 'Fear was the main impression left upon my mind, and pain upon my body (being generally kicked by big lower-boy Oppidans both before and after school) ... the distance to his [Warre's] schoolroom afforded only too great an opportunity to my tormentors – sometimes I dream of them even now.'[3] Thus, at fifty years distance, an old Colleger recalls his own experience.

The oppression of the small, clever, sensitive young Colleger by the hulking oafs who only came to Eton because they were rich or well-born is a stereotype that tempts the righteous indignation in us all. Certainly many such instances could be cited from the nineteenth and even some from the twentieth century. But it is unsafe to project it too far into the past. In the first place it was not until 1844 that election to a scholarship at Eton began to depend on evidence of academic ability. In that historic year four candidates were actually rejected: previously it had been a matter of nomination. Exactly how this worked is not fully known but the main outlines are clear enough. If the King or some great figure in the state indicated their preference for some particular candidate it would be rash in the Provost and Fellows to disregard it. They had, of course, their own fish to fry. And

3 C.R.L. Fletcher *Edmond Warre* (1922), 77.

they would naturally be disposed to pay attention to the recommendations of distinguished churchmen or heads of houses at Oxford or Cambridge.

College might then not unfairly be characterised as part of an enclosed system of status and privilege. Yet even in the very early days of the foundation there is evidence of its having opened a career to the talents. We have seen that the statutes forbade entry to serfs. In 1469 a villein on one of the College estates in Dorset was given his freedom and, at the age of fourteen, elected a scholar of Eton.[4] He went on to King's two years later and after he had been ordained priest returned to Eton as one of the chaplains or conducts as they are called. Like the great majority of his contemporaries, gentle or simple, cleric or layman, he died young. There are many other instances in succeeding centuries of the sons of tradesmen and artisans being admitted to College but there is not before 1844 any presumptive reason to suppose that they were necessarily cleverer or of a more academic cast of mind than their Oppidan contemporaries. But if they were, College opened the prospect of a learned career.

In the confrontation between the little Colleger and the Oppidan bullies it was remarked that Collegers were not necessarily smaller in physique. In fact historically the probability is that, on average, the Colleger was taller and stronger. The reason for this is that their average age was much higher. They stayed on longer at school because they, and they alone, stood to profit from any vacancies that might occur at King's. Only when they had passed the age of 20 were they disqualified for entry into that lush pasture where they might feed for the rest of their lives. Oppidans left much earlier: they had no comparable motive for staying on. Until the Victorian reforms changed the system the biggest and strongest boys were mostly Collegers. The evidence of this leaps to the eye in the early history of Eton cricket. Collegers always took up a disproportionate number of places in the Eleven – in one year no less than eight. In the annual cricket match against the Oppidans College, drawing on

4 *Etoniana* 51/9.

an average of fifty boys as against four or five hundred, usually won. It would be an inspiration to intellectual pursuits if this result could be attributed to the triumph of brain over brawn. But the Colleger of the late eighteenth or early nineteenth century was hardly to be thought of as an intellectual in the making. This account recollected by one who had been in College from 1787 to 1793 suggests the personality of Mr Jingle rather than that of George Orwell or Aldous Huxley:

'I had continually Horses lent me by a Friend at Windsor ... On one occasion met with another Boy Lord Berkeley's Hounds from Cranford Bridge at Sydenham Copse – chopped a Vixen – the Dog took us over Chalvey ditch to Salt hill – black Park – almost to Beaconsfield – back to Burnham Beeches – ran short there – Bulstrode Park – long check there – the Fox seen by a Farmer between two fat hog's shoulders – a very good run – got a pad – knew I should be flogged – two Praeposters (*Sic*) [Prefects] waiting to seize me at my Dames – galloped thro' Eton – the Masters at dinner – was seized and Dr Davies waiting at home to flog me; had my desert before dinner – five or six to meet us at the Christopher – Mr Kendal's superexcellent Port to drink success to Foxhunting ...'[5]

And so on. The author goes on to recall with particular zest a fight between two boys that had lasted an hour and a half. The indiscipline, the brutality, the exaltation of physical courage as the single and supreme virtue, the sheer mindlessness of the unreformed public school tumble pell mell from this and many other such accounts of Eton life. It was at its toughest and coarsest in College. The sensitive, the conscientious and the intelligent were likely to be much better off as Oppidans.

The Founder had clearly intended that his scholars should live plainly, even austerely, but he had made ample provision for them to live decently. By the eighteenth century their conditions had become so squalid that, as has already been pointed out, it was no longer possible to find enough candidates to fill the vacancies. Even so robust a figure as the Colleger just

5 *Etoniana* 22/350.

quoted refers to being seized 'at my Dame's', that is, at his lodging house in the town. He was not, like an Oppidan, allowed to sleep there but he evidently spent most of his day there beginning with breakfast which, unbelievably, the Governing Body did not provide for the growing boys under their care until they were forced to by the unwelcome publicity of a Parliamentary Commission. As Edward Coleridge, later son-in-law to the formidable Dr Keate and himself a master and subsequently Fellow of Eton, succinctly put it:

'Life in Long Chamber in my time [he went to Eton in 1813] was a very rough one, and too severe a trial for any Boy. It was neither Moral, Decent or Cleanly ... Such food as we had was badly cooked and ill-served. The College provided neither Breakfast nor Tea, nor any eatable supper. There were no means of washing for any but the Sixth Form [the ten most senior Collegers], and those of the meanest sort, and provided by their Fags ... All were locked up after Latin Prayers in the Lower School at 8.30, and left to themselves or the tender mercies of the Sixth Form till 7 a.m. next morning ... there were many things done, which one cannot but remember with horror and regret. And yet there was a kind of safety in the indecent Publicity of our Lives: and in our numbers were the grounds of much pleasant converse, amusement, and Friendship.' Coleridge incidentally confirms the evidence of his fox-hunting predecessor of twenty years earlier: 'We all had rooms in the town, where we spent the day, breakfasted and had tea, which two meals we provided ourselves.'[6]

The dirt, the discomfort and the filthy food were disgraceful enough. But what chills the blood is the thought of those interminable nights of bullying and beastliness. One favourite amusement was tossing in the blanket. In 1828 a small boy, tossed high in the air, missed the blanket and fell with his head on the corner of a heavy iron-bound oak bedstead 'the result of which was that he was completely *scalped*, as with a tomahawk, the scalp hanging down over the neck and back, suspended only by a small piece of skin ... By a merciful providence, it was

6 *Etoniana* 81/483.

found that neither was the skull fractured, nor was there a concussion of the brain; indeed, beyond the pain of having the scalp sewn on again, and the natural irritation of the wound, he did not at all suffer either at the time, or in after life.'[7] In fact he went on to become a distinguished Sanskrit scholar and to write a work on Christianity and Hinduism that was admired throughout the learned world. Tossing in the blanket, we are told, was discontinued for some years. But there is no evidence that the Head Master or the Governing Body felt any of those anxieties of conscience that were to trouble them so sorely when their own position or emoluments were subject to the rude inquiries of a Parliamentary Commission only a few years later.

7 *Etoniana* 43/673.

CHAPTER TWO

On the Map of Learning

THE SERENITY OF ANCIENT BUILDINGS rejects ideas of the harsh, the mean and the squalid. In a cathedral close the iniquities of medieval society do not press themselves on the consciousness. Can it be that the colleges of Oxford and Cambridge, so airy, so dignified, so well-preserved, were in the eighteenth century mere clubhouses for the sottish idlers that Gibbon so unforgettably describes? Yet no one who has not seen and felt what every unprejudiced visitor to such places sees and feels can grasp the simple fact that comprehends so many complexities and reconciles so many apparently irreconcilables, namely that the past was once the present. Bristling as it is with inconsistencies, uncertainties, contradictions and questions in their very nature unanswerable, we know that we can never sum up, define or explain the world in which we live. That plenty of people are ready to do so makes no matter. Simple explanations of what we know to be illimitably complicated are not convincing. We employ our minds and our imaginations to understand as much as we can.

So it is with the past of a great and continuing institution. Beauty and ugliness, dignity and squalor co-exist and do not cancel each other out. Broadly speaking the life led by Etonians from the fifteenth century to the nineteenth was harsh, ill-regulated and unhealthy. Violence, drunkenness and indiscipline were sometimes contained but were never far away. At least that seems to be the weight of the surviving evidence, most of it from the later and thus notably gentler and softer part of the period. In the matter of health Eton was no worse, perhaps even rather better, than its times. Medicine was everywhere a hazard rather than a help. Diet was generally misunderstood: ill-balanced not only in its components but in the times of meals and the quantities provided. The use of alcohol was unwise. Up to 1890 the Collegers had the right on summer afternoons to unlimited beer for themselves and such boys as they might invite to share their privilege in College Hall. Such a statutory inducement to intemperance can hardly have been intended by the Founder. Even more extraordinary was the permission of a public house, the Christopher Inn, right in the very heart of Eton. Though technically out of bounds to the boys it was in fact the scene of constant excess and a source of huge profit to its successive proprietors. Drunkenness was too common a characteristic of society at all levels and at all ages for it to cause the disgust and alarm that parents and masters would feel nowadays. If diet was not understood, if doctoring generally did more harm than good, sanitation was scarcely attempted. Here at least the great founders were ahead of their age in their heroic confrontation of a problem almost everywhere neglected. William of Wykeham's solution was characteristically architectural. At Oxford he erected a large building, completely detached from the rest of his college, with latrines on the first floor. The whole groundfloor was an enormous cess-pit. Henry VI's design at Eton though less monumental was more modern. A great sewer was constructed, to be cleared by a periodic discharge of water that carried off everything into the Thames. This of course served only the buildings of the original foundation centred on School Yard.

In such a detail the resemblance to the monasteries comes easily to mind. If the first century of Eton with its emphasis on a strict daily routine revolving round the devotional offices reminds us of the pioneering days of Western monasticism it is not after all surprising because King Henry was trying to do for his day what the founders of the abbeys had done for theirs. As with the abbeys in the early middle ages the austerity that we find so striking was not so marked by contrast with the world outside. A hundred years later when the abbeys, latterly rich and flushed with good living, had been suppressed, Elizabethan Eton still retained an air of strictness and piety, of what was already beginning to be called Puritanism. But the worldliness and eccentricity that were to form such conspicuous features of its character were already breaking in. Nicholas Udall who was twice Head Master under Henry VIII was author of the first surviving comedy written in English, *Ralph Roister Doister*. He encouraged theatricals at the school and evidently had considerable talents as a producer since he was employed in this capacity first by Anne Boleyn and then, incredibly, by Queen Mary. Like Dr Keate three centuries later he was a legend in his own day for flogging. That he was exceptionally gifted and obviously disreputable is the one clear judgment that can be made of him. He was involved with two of the boys in stealing some of the College plate and in the course of the subsequent inquiry confessed to having had homosexual relations with one of them. How he extricated himself from all this and even secured from Eton the arrears of his salary we can only wonder. He crowned an inexplicable career by being appointed Head Master of Westminster by the deeply pious and strongly conservative Queen Mary. Admittedly she suppressed the foundation a year later but there is nothing to suggest that Udall who had made his career as a fashionable Protestant intellectual had in any way forfeited her favour.

Udall introduces two notes into Eton that have been heard there again: raffishness and plausibility. It was hardly possible that an institution so close to the court and to the life of fashion could keep itself unspotted from the world. Whatever criticism has been levelled at the place it has never been accused of being too much concerned with respectability. There is an extravagance, an originality, about Udall that distracts the eye from his all too evident unfitness for the position he so strangely occupied.

More typical of the calculating worldliness that elbows its

way to success was the Provost* who held office for almost the whole of Elizabeth's reign, William Day. Like Udall he seems to have helped himself to the College plate but to have managed matters more discreetly. Day always took good care to avoid compromising himself. His elder brother as Provost of King's had secured his election to Eton and thus to a Fellowship at his own College by the age of nineteen. The younger Day annoyed the elder by taking the Protestant side in the controversies of the Reformation but not so obdurately as to risk his Fellowship when Queen Mary brought back the old religion. On Queen Elizabeth's accession he took holy orders. Within a year of being made priest he had acquired a rich portfolio of preferments, securing the Provostship against hot competition largely by virtue of being unmarried. Once established in the post he lost no time in marrying into the family that above all others seemed to have the knack of picking up bishoprics. His father-in-law and all his four brothers-in-law enjoyed or were to enjoy that condition. Day did his best to join them but it was only at the very end of his life that he at last succeeded one of them in the see of Winchester. During his thirty-four years at Eton he had piled up such an aggregation of deaneries, canonries and rich benefices that only an exceptionally well-endowed bishopric would have made it worth his while to move.

Day's career, at first sight imposing but undistinguished by any achievement, exemplifies much that can be observed in the subsequent success of many Etonians. He owed his start to family connexion and improved his position by the same means. When Elizabeth made England safe for Protestantism he showed great enthusiasm in obliterating or destroying the stained glass and the wall-paintings of the College chapel.

---

* A note on the respective roles of Provost and Head Master may here be of help. The Provost was (and still is) Head of the Governing Body, which consists of himself and the Fellows. With them he shares a general responsibility for the well-being of the College (including its finances and its buildings). His personal duties have in the course of time come to resemble those of a constitutional monarch rather than those of a chief executive. He regulates the services in chapel and, with the rest of the Governing Body, appoints the Head Master, who has always been in charge of teaching and school administration. In unreformed Eton the Provost enjoyed a larger salary than the Head Master. Now the position is reversed.

He presided competently and affably over the foundation. No scholar himself, he appointed Head Masters who maintained a decent standard. Bland, empty, courteous and grasping he was not to lack for imitators in the centuries that followed.

The Eton over which he ruled witnessed the beginnings of a fissure, latter to be magnified into a Grand Canyon, between the scholars and the Fellows. Life for a scholar was Spartan, his education stiff and narrow, his amusements few and for the most part brutal. Under Dr Day the Fellows began to taste the pleasures of increasing wealth and diminishing responsibilities. Early in his time they obtained a relaxation of the statute that forbade them to hold a living in addition to their Fellowship. As rich absentees they were less likely to concern themselves, still less to identify themselves, with the *lumpenproletariat* of scholars from which they sprang. A Fellowship at Eton became rarer and richer. Rarer because there were now few incentives to resign; a Deanery, a Bishopric, the Provostship of Eton or King's, but not much else. Richer because the value of the endowment rose with the general growth of the economy. Thus a Fellowship came more and more to be thought of as a thing to be coveted and less and less as an active position in a great school. By the eighteenth century the separation was complete. The Provost and Fellows annexed to themselves the huge increase that three hundred years had brought to the College revenues while leaving the scholars in the poverty and squalor of the middle ages.

Under the Stuarts these processes were arrested, largely because the foundation came under the influence of two of the most learned and intellectually energetic Provosts in its history, Sir Henry Savile and Sir Henry Wotton. Both were scholars with a European reputation. Savile had been Warden of Merton College, Oxford, and continued to hold the post during the quarter of a century that he was Provost of Eton. He was only the second layman to be appointed in flat contradiction of the statutory requirement that the Provost should be in priest's orders. The aging Elizabeth hesitated long before granting the necessary dispensation but Savile had a great deal on his side. He had been appointed Greek tutor to the Queen some twenty years after her accession when she had neither time nor need for mere pedagogic instruction and had served her in a diplomatic capacity during his continental travels. He was championed by Essex, the greatest of Royal favourites. He was rich and had no scruples about offering bribes. He was notably handsome and had a fine presence. He knew what he wanted and he meant to get it. Once established at Eton, the full force of that autocratic personality before which the Fellows of Merton had quailed was turned on the ingrown and provincial institution that had settled into an unambitious monotony. Savile was intent on propelling Eton from its comfortable backwater into the main stream of scholarship. His first act was to refurbish the library and move it to more spacious quarters. During his tenure of office he built it up on a generous and carefully considered plan, strengthening its holdings in the Greek and Latin authors, both ancient and Christian, and developing those in theology and history and Civil Law. More ambitiously Savile determined to make Eton a centre of learned printing and set up a press from which in due course issued his own critical edition of the works of St John Chrysostom in eight volumes folio. The Greek types which he acquired to print it were also used in two smaller works, negligible in themselves but landmarks as being among the earliest examples of Greek printing in England. To accommodate his press he built what was one of the most attractive of all Eton houses until a bomb landed on it in 1940 disturbing the present writer from his pursuit of the classical studies that Savile had so nobly endowed.

It was not only buildings, presses and Greek types (subsequently presented to the University of Oxford) with which the new Provost enriched the foundation. He gathered round him a circle of scholars and in doing so gave to Eton a quality that it has never since entirely lost, the sense of belonging to the world of the university. Among them was the greatest Greek scholar in England, John Hales, to whom Clarendon, who knew him well, attributes the real credit for Savile's Chrysostom. If true, it would be characteristic because Hales's generosity and self-effacement are attested by every contemporary source. He had the natural, easy accessibility to simple unintellectual people that three centuries later made the Provost of the inter-war years, M.R. James, so widely beloved and so long remembered. He wrote very little but what he did write, and what he was, gave English scholarship a large measure of its distinctive excellence. The historian of classical scholarship, Professor Rudolf Pfeiffer, singles him out for particular praise in transmitting the tradition of Christian Platonic humanism that he finds 'especially characteristic of England . . . John Hales imbued even his contributions to theological controversy with charm and humanity.'[1] John Aubrey has left an imperishably vivid sketch of him taken within a year of his death: '. . . a prettie little man, sanguine, of a cheerfull countenance, very gentile and courteous; I was received by him with much humanity: he was in a kind of violet-coloured cloath Gowne, with buttons and loopes (he wore not a black gowne) and was reading Thomas à Kempis . . .'[2]

This interview took place at Eton of which Hales had been made a Fellow in 1613, although like Savile himself he was an Oxford man with no Etonian antecedents. But if he was not formed by the place he did as much as any man, with the possible exception of William Johnson Cory two centuries later, to articulate and express its peculiar virtues. Like Cory, Hales did not allow his profound classical scholarship to unbalance his judgment of the ancient authors by diminishing the moderns. His taste was original, not to say daring:

'Mr Hales of Eton affirmed that he would show all the poets of antiquity outdone by Shakespeare, in all the topics and commonplaces made use of in poetry. The enemies of Shakespeare would by no means yield him so much excellence, so that it came to a resolution of a trial of skill upon that subject. The place agreed on for the dispute was Mr Hales's chamber at Eton. A great many books were sent down by the enemies of this poet, and on the appointed day my Lord Falkland, Sir John Suckling, and all the persons of quality that had wit and learning and interested themselves in the quarrel met there, and upon

1 Pfeiffer, *History of Classical Scholarship from 1300 to 1850* (Oxford, 1976), 144.
2 *Brief Lives* ed. Lawson Dick (3rd edition, 1958), 117.

a thorough disquisition of the point, the judges chosen by agreement out of this learned and ingenious assembly unanimously gave the preference to Shakespeare.'[3]

Hales was more than a century ahead of his time in recognising the highest genius. For this one great, glorious critical insight he would deserve the title 'ever memorable' which was long and affectionately applied to him. Aubrey tells us that 'When the Court was at Windsor, the learned Courtiers much delighted in his company.' Even more than his learning and his penetration of judgment, his beauty of character was the focus of attraction. 'Mr Hales was the common Godfather there, and 'twas pretty to see, as he walked to Windsor, how his Godchildren fell on their knees. When he was Bursar, he still gave away all his Groates for the Acquittances [a petty cash payment made on the settling of an account] to his Godchildren; and by that time he came to Windsor bridge, he would have never a Groat left.'

This description of perhaps the most exemplary figure in the history of Eton, is the more telling because Aubrey had no personal connexion with the place. Hales's life, if anyone's, expressed the 'religion and sound learning' to which the foundation was directed. Henry VI would have approved his bounty to the village children as he made his way up Eton High Street. Yet like Savile, who appointed him, and Henry Wotton, who was Provost for the fifteen years between the accession of Charles I and the first distant thunder of approaching Civil War, Hales had travelled in Europe and knew the world. In this he personifies an aspect of Eton in the life of the country that any modern reader would recognise.

Sir Henry Wotton who completes this trio of scholars whose fame reached far beyond their own country and their own age combines some of the qualities of the other two. Like Savile he was a younger son of an aristocratic family, born and brought up to a condition of life that required either wealth or exertion for its support. Both had in some degree a worldliness, an eye to the main chance, of which Hales was innocent. On the other

3 Dryden, *Works* (ed. Saintsbury) XV, 344 quot. Maxwell-Lyte, 228.

hand Wotton, like Hales, was a wit as well as a man of learning. His classic definition of an ambassador as a man sent to lie abroad for the good of his country nearly cost him his career when it came to the ears of King James in whose name he had been accredited to the Republic of Venice. Savile, according to Aubrey, 'could not abide Witts: when a young Scholar was recommended to him for a good Witt, "Out upon him, I'le having nothing to doe with him; give me the ploding student. If I would look for witts, I would goe to Newgate: there be the Witts." ' Like Hales too Wotton was both a poet and a Christian who would have nothing to do with the religious antagonisms that were tearing Europe in pieces. 'The itch for controversy is the eczema of the Church' is the epitaph he chose for his gravestone. Less magnificent than Savile, less saintly than Hales, Izaak Walton has left a charming picture of this pipe-smoking fellow-angler whose Provostship consolidated and enriched what Savile had begun. Between the death of Elizabeth and the outbreak of the Civil War Eton had become a placename on the map of the learned world.

How complete was its acceptance as a national institution the Civil War soon showed. Wotton's successor as Provost, Dr Steward, one of Charles I's most trusted servants who had joined his master immediately the Royal Standard was raised at Nottingham, was deprived by Parliament and replaced by a Puritan, Francis Rous. But there was no question of confiscating the endowments of the College, still less of suppressing it. Even the Fellows, Royalists to a man, were not turned out until they refused to take the Engagement, or oath of loyalty to the Commonwealth, in 1649. Hales, survivor of the great days, was urged to reconcile himself to the new government so that he might continue to enjoy his Fellowship but refused, selling his superb collection of books at less than a third of its value so that he might have something to live on. His kind old landlady told Aubrey 'that she was much against the sale of 'em, because she knew it was his Life and joy'. The war and the overturning of the old order in Church and State interrupted the smooth running of the twin foundations of Eton and King's but did not bring them to a halt. Indeed once Cromwell was firmly in the saddle the school, like the ancient universities, enjoyed a period of tolerant prosperity that was reflected in the comparatively easy transition that followed Charles II's restoration in 1660. If Hales could not be persuaded to resume his Fellowship on terms his conscience could not approve, he was yet allowed to live in the shadow of the chapel he loved (though not to worship there) and to be buried, as he asked, in its graveyard. The Head Master appointed by Provost Rous was dismissed at the Restoration, only to be succeeded by the Lower Master*. Continuity had in all essentials been preserved.

The only change and that a small one in the social structure of the school was the disappearance of the Commensals, those sons of noblemen who by the Founder's provision were admitted to a status resembling that of a Gentleman Commoner at the university. From this time on Etonians have been divided into Collegers and Oppidans. One of the last of the Commensals who was among the most brilliant minds ever to have been educated at Eton has left an attractive sketch of his time there. Robert Boyle, one of the founders of the Royal Society and a figure of the first importance in the development of science, was at Eton from 1635 to 1639. He has given one of the earliest accounts of what can be seen as the most valuable and characteristic element, sometimes obscured or diminished but never eroded, in the Eton tradition: its individualism and its informality.

'... his master, Mr *Harrison*, taking notice of some aptness and much willingness in him to learn, resolved to improve them both by all the gentlest ways of encouragement; for he would often dispense from his attendance at school, at the accustomed hours, to instruct him privately and familiarly in his chamber ... He would sometimes give him unasked play-days, and oft bestow upon him such balls, and tops, and other implements of idleness, as he had taken away from others, that had unduly used them. He would sometimes commend others before him, to rouse his emulation, and oftentimes give him commendations before others, to engage his endeavours to deserve them.

* see p. 203.

Not to be tedious, he was careful to instruct him in such an affable kind and gentle way, that he easily prevailed with him to consider studying, not so much as a duty of obedience to his superiors, but as the way to purchase for himself a most delightful and invaluable good. In effect, he soon created in *Philaretus* [Boyle's name for himself] so strong a passion to acquire knowledge, that what time he could spare from a scholar's task, which his retentive memory made him not find uneasy, he would usually employ so greedily in reading, that his master would sometimes be necessitated to force him out to play, on which, and upon study, he looked as if their natures were inverted. But that which .. first .. made him so passionate a friend to reading was the accidental perusal of *Quintus Curtius* [a Latin historian who wrote an account of the life of Alexander the Great], which first made him in love with other than pedantick books and conjured up in him that unsatisfied appetite of knowledge, that is yet as greedy as when it first was raised ...'[4]

Boyle, as a Commensal and the son of one of Sir Henry Wotton's oldest friends, can hardly be cited as a typical Eton boy of his period. It is difficult to imagine him taking part in the baiting of animals, or the fighting that seem to have been such common sources of enjoyment. And the life of a Colleger, lived in Long Chamber, can hardly have offered the opportunities for reading at large and following one's own interests that Boyle so agreeably describes.

Altogether, the seventeenth century was a fortunate and creative one for Eton. The Provost of Charles II's time, Richard Allestree, and the Head Master, John Newborough, who was appointed in 1690, were both exemplary. Allestree who was Regius Professor of Divinity at Oxford was closely associated with Dean Fell in his virtual refounding of the Oxford University Press. Newborough, who had been a Colleger during Allestree's time, founded a school library for the use of the boys. In his will he left his own copy of *Purchas his Pilgrimes*, the great text of English exploration and adventure overseas, to the future Prime Minister, Sir Robert Walpole, who had been in

4 Robert Boyle *Collected Works* (1744) reprinted in *Etoniana*, 7/109.

College in the first years of his headmastership. Allestree and Newborough at the end of the century, less famous than Savile and Wotton at the beginning, maintained and extended what they had done to make Eton renowned for polite learning. In Newborough's friendship with old pupils, St John, Wyndham, Walpole, who were making their mark in the House of Commons another connexion characteristic of Eton can be seen in the forming. Politics and politicians touch the imagination, excite the enthusiasms of Eton in the nineteenth and twentieth centuries as perhaps in no other English school. There are always a large number of boys whose fathers are active politicians and who are therefore accustomed to hearing the subject talked about by people who know their way about the political world. That world, turning on the poles of Parliament and Party, was born in the struggles of the seventeenth century. In Newborough's time it was still young. But it gave to the classical studies that monopolised the curriculum up to Victorian times and still dominated it thereafter a new aptness and point. The Greeks and the Romans took it for granted that civilized and educated people would be interested in public affairs; indeed that they would be unworthy of their citizenship if they were not. Classical literature is saturated with political ideas. The essential character of Eton may not have been discernible by the end of the seventeenth century but its chief components were already assembled.

CHAPTER THREE

———∿———

The Rough with the Smooth

THE SMOOTHNESS SO OFTEN pointed out as a distasteful feature of Etonian manners and mentality comes in, as it came in so many departments of English life, in the eighteenth century. It is the nature of smoothness to belong to a surface: most of the boys who went to the school found the substance rough enough. But smoothness is also a function of stability, the quality that dominated the politics and the society of Georgian England and is so happily expressed in its architecture. It is a quality not likely to be undervalued in an age such as ours where it seems to be in diminishing supply. But it is possible to have too much of a good thing. Eton in the eighteenth century was not merely stable: it was static.

This is to speak of its ideas, its purposes and its intellectual life. Its indiscipline, its rowdiness, its violence erupted fitfully into lawlessness or even rebellion. The most famous of these outbreaks occurred in 1768 when a hundred and sixty boys threw their books in the river (except for one who refused to part with his Homer) and marched off to Maidenhead. Authority became more and more precarious as, with growing prosperity, numbers rose without a corresponding increase in the number of masters. Size governs so much else. From the foundation to the Civil War the school can hardly at the best of times have reached as high a figure as 150 and must often have been very much smaller. The earliest school list is that for 1678, well on into the Provostship of Richard Allestree, who metaphorically and literally built up the school (Upper School, the handsome entrance block that forms the western side of School Yard, is

his most conspicuous monument). The total then, even including nine boys who had just left, is still only 207. Thereafter until
the reforming era of the 1840s and 1850s numbers fluctuate in
response, so far as can be seen, to the quality of the Head
Master. After the Allestree-Newborough epoch numbers
reached a peak of 416 in 1720. A run of less distinguished
successors brought them down to 265 in 1739. The appointment in 1754 of Dr Edward Barnard, by far the most successful
and respected of the eighteenth century Head Masters, inspired
a dramatic recovery. On his elevation to the Provostship in 1765
the numbers stood at 552, a total not again approached until the
latter part of Keate's time, some sixty years later. Barnard's
successor was a disaster. Within three years he had provoked
the rebellion already referred to. Within ten the numbers had
sunk to 246.

To maintain even a semblance of order among several hundred children, adolescents and young men ranging in age from
eight to nearly twenty, many of them rich and allowed to run
wild, required nerve, tact and judgment. It cannot have been
easy even in the classroom, if it is not misleading to apply such
a term to the magnificent but hardly intimate setting in which
the Head Master and three or four assistants laboured to instruct two or three hundred Upper Boys in Latin and Greek.
Outside there was little formal attempt to do so. The masters
were too thin on the ground. Dr Barnard's first act had been to
increase the staff by two. As the numbers grew with his success
he appointed two more, but this was to palliate rather than to
cure. The houses in which the Oppidans lived were only loosely
controlled by the school authorities whose sovereignty was
theoretically acknowledged. Their proprietors, originally land-
ladies and thus known as 'dames', were often teachers of extra-
curricular subjects, writing masters, music masters, drawing
masters, teachers of fencing and dancing. The assistants, as the
masters employed to *assist* the Head Master were termed, were
expressly forbidden to keep boarding houses though they were
allowed to have a few pupils living with them. By the end of the
eighteenth century this vague relaxation had been silently extended. By the early nineteenth it had submerged the original

prohibition. The framework of the housemaster system on which all public schools have long been organised thus came into being, a ready instrument for the reform and development of the Victorian age. The house and the housemaster in many schools and for many boys transcended the school itself.

Not so in the eighteenth century. The disciplinary theory of the public schools of the *ancien régime* made a virtue of inadequacy. There were not enough masters to keep up even a pretence of a rational, civilized and orderly course of life outside the hours of school and chapel – in both of which scenes of hooliganism were far from rare. By advancing the argument that to leave the boys to organise their own government was to educate them in manliness and to fire them with the love of freedom, a case could be made for leaving matters as they were. The boys would learn what the world was really like. And, being true-born, high-bred Britons they would naturally prefer being badly governed by themselves to being well governed by somebody else. Limitations as to bounds and times, prohibitions as to drinking, gambling and other undesirable pursuits were laid down to be enforced by flogging or expulsion but the policing of these regulations depended almost entirely on the senior boys. If, as they often did, they granted themselves a liberal dispensation in these matters that was no doubt regrettable: but provided that open scandal was avoided no action was called for.

Even the much admired Dr Barnard professed no high expectation of virtuous conduct from the boys entrusted to his care. 'So young and yet so wicked' was a maxim of experience attributed to him by an old pupil.[1] In contrast to Dr Arnold at Rugby in the next century he appears resigned to the acceptance of moral evil. Belabouring a young nobleman for getting a girl with child he is said to have exclaimed 'after some few lashes – "Psha! what signifies my flogging him for being like his father? What's bred in the bone will never get out of the flesh." '[2] The Head Master and his assistants had often to overcome the

1 *Etoniana* 20/320.
2 *ibid*, 19/293.

handicap of humble origins in their efforts to control boys who might not have learned any idea of discipline but had certainly developed a consciousness of rank. Barnard's unpopular successor was the son of a local tradesman. Even as late as the 1860s the Head Master, Dr Balston, had been adjured by his father to remember always that he was not a gentleman.[3] The Head Master and his assistants were throughout the period drawn exclusively from those who had themselves been in College where the horrors of life were such that vacancies were often left unfilled. The sons of tradesmen and artisans had more incentive to endure such a grisly initiation to a life of learned ease than those whose means made such miseries unnecessary. Nonetheless the well-to-do, and even peers, sometimes subjected their children to this ordeal for the chance of seeing them permanently settled in life with at the very least a Fellowship at King's. There, if they did not die of drink as two of the Fellows did within four months in 1748,[4] there would be oportunities of doing a great deal better.

The issue is well summed up in a letter of Thomas Gray, Eton's poet laureate, written in 1761:

> My notion is that your Nephew being an only Son, & rather of a delicate constitution, ought not to be exposed to the hardships of the College. I know that the expense in that way is much lessen'd; but your Brother has but one Son, & can afford to breed him an Oppidant. I know, that a Colleger is sooner formed to scuffle in the world, that is, by drubbing & tyranny is made more hardy or more cunning, but these in my eyes are no such desirable acquisitions: I know too, that a certain (or very probable) provision for life is a thing to be wished: but you must remember what a thing a fellow of King's is.[5]

Gray stresses the harshness of a Colleger's life but that of an Oppidan, softer and less squalid in its conditions, was yet exposed to a degree of violence that we should find horrifying. Fighting was both the great test of social acceptability and an approved form of physical recreation. Organised

3 A.C. Ainger, *Eton Sixty Years Ago* (1917), 230.
4 *Etoniana* 95/712.
5 *Letters of Thos. Gray* ed. Tovey, ii, 215.

games were unknown. Some cricket was played; there was rowing and swimming; the Wall Game, the most brutish and least elegant mutation of football to have survived into the present day, dates from this period and may be taken as an authentic expression of its spirit. The age, for all its veneer of social grace and intellectual enlightenment, was still by our standards violent. Rape and assault were among the most common causes of legal action. Streets were neither lighted nor policed. It could plausibly be argued that every man ought to be trained to defend himself.

Nonetheless the level of violence tacitly accepted by the authorities at Eton far exceeded any such requirement. In December 1784 the *London Chronicle* printed an account of a fight between two Eton boys in which one had been killed and the other seriously hurt. A verdict of accidental death was brought in and the victim 'was interred in Eton College Church. All the Gentlemen of the school attended his funeral.' The most famous of such incidents took place during Keate's headmastership in 1825 when Lord Shaftesbury's youngest son was killed in a fight lasting two hours. Keate apparently thought that the senior boys who were watching the fight were much to blame in not stopping it. But no one was punished. Keate himself was not held in any way responsible for what had happened: and the only strongly expressed opinion was the universal approval of Lord Shaftesbury for not bringing an action for manslaughter against the boy who had killed his son.[6] The event was felt to be shocking but no blame was attributable. Had Darwin's theory of Natural Selection been available at the time it would no doubt have been urged in support.

For this was the real core of the moral defence: grim, harsh, cruel as the system might be it prevented the evils of softness, of effeminacy, of degeneration. Whether such dangers were exaggerated, whether, even if they were as real as they were made out, they still might prove a more acceptable risk, were questions that scarcely anyone asked. It was axiomatic that softness and comfort destroyed courage and spirit. In the late Victorian period almost all housemasters still refused to allow

6 *Etoniana* 14/208, 15/225; 90/632.

armchairs in the boys' rooms. Indeed in some houses this ban remained in force in the 1920s and 1930s. At the turn of the eighteenth century a far more extreme view was generally accepted. 'Sawneyness' as the habit of soft living was called was deplored by intellectuals and aesthetes as much as by those who lived for field sports. If the Duke of Wellington's often quoted remark that the battle of Waterloo was won on the playing fields of Eton is authentic it must be remembered that in his day there were no organised games. The playing fields were the arena in which the boys fought each other.

Naturally this uncontrolled behaviour often overflowed the loosely drawn and feebly manned frontiers of the school to become a general public nuisance. The poorer inhabitants of Windsor and Eton were liable to find themselves involved in the fisticuffs in which the boys took such an exuberant delight. Fights with the bargees using the river were common. Sometimes the boys picked on a man who was prepared to claim legal redress as was the case when they set on Sir Robert Rich's coachman in 1753. His master helped him fight his action to a successful conclusion, but the character of Eton as a school for the rich and the powerful must have cowed those who knew they were neither.

The ostentatious style of life adopted by Charles James Fox was held by contemporaries to have influenced the tone of the place. Fox was in the school in Barnard's time when Eton was booming so that it seems too precise to attribute so wide a change to a single boy, popular, fashionable and talented though he was. It was Barnard who began the practice of inviting boys to present their portraits to the Head Master on taking leave of him, in lieu of the substantial cash donative that since the end of the seventeenth century had become one of the established perquisites of the post. The wealth of England was growing rapidly in the second half of the eighteenth century and the urbane figures who presided over Eton were alert to secure their share. Scholarship was not forgotten. The boys received a grounding in Latin and Greek grammar that made slovenliness of language and cloudiness of thought uneasy to them. And they often acquired, as Fox himself did, a love of ancient literature that lasted all their lives. The magnificent library, reserved for the Provost and Fellows, had been finished in 1729 and continued to extend its holdings throughout the century, culminating in the bequest in 1799 of one of the greatest private collections ever formed in England. The man who made it had been a pupil of Barnard's.

Great libraries do not grow, the love of books does not take root, in places where there is no life of the mind. Eighteenth century Eton, for all its barbarity, for all its stink of money, remembered its vocation to sound learning. But when running one's eye down the list of Georgian Provosts one sees Dr Bland succeeded by Dr Sleech one catches Nature in the act of imitating Art. The long succession of comfortable divines, heaving themselves into stertorous activity when a canonry at Windsor falls vacant or there is a choice piece of preferment for a son-in-law and then relapsing into a more decorous torpor, presents an uninspiring spectacle. Uninspiring because they were themselves uninspired. The learning may have been sound but it had become mechanical. Not, indeed, in the literal sense of that word. The curriculum did not alter in the slightest degree from the beginning of the century to the end. Wars were fought: an empire was won in India and another was lost in America: the voyages of Captain Cook extended the limits of the world: the French Revolution engulfed the states and societies of Europe. But Eton took no cognizance of these transformations.

It had not been so in the first two and a half centuries of its existence. It was not to be so in the Victorian age. Schools, particularly boarding schools, are by their nature inclined to keep the outside world at a distance. Like any other tightly knit community they form a world of their own and are, in the medieval phrase, a cause unto themselves. But the insularity of Eton, a danger more recurrent as the place grew richer and more conscious of its importance, achieved by the turn of the eighteenth and nineteenth centuries the solid, four-square firmness of Georgian architecture.

Why was this? A prickly Scotsman visiting Eton in the seventeen-eighties as private tutor to the young Lord

Tullibardine then in the school dismisses the masters as 'all so rich, so purse-proud and so much addicted to allow consequence to a man only in proportion to his rank in the Church, that a poor and proud Presbyterian cannot be greatly liked ... The question there is not "What are his attainments? Is he ingenuous?" but "Is he an Etonian? Is he entered at King's College? What views [i.e. prospects] of preferment has he?" '7 The closed circuit of Eton and King's, the easy circumstances awaiting the privileged entrants, explain much. Clearly nothing must be done that might disturb that felicitous arrangement. The rising tide of wealth and fashion on which it floated had however the contrary effect of lowering the Head Master and his assistants in their own self-respect. There is a flunkeyism about their behaviour at its most unmistakable in the Head Master's readiness to accept, even by swift establishment of custom to require, a leaving present in cash. A Head Master ought to be distinguishable from a headwaiter. Besides 'leaving money', as it was called, a capitation fee not allowed for in the statutes was also charged (four guineas a year for ordinary Oppidans and double for a nobleman). Other arbitrary extortions such as an entrance fee swelled his receipts. The College that Henry VI had founded had become a lucrative corporation, jealous of its privileges and obdurate to innovation.

It was during the headmastership (1809 – 34) of Keate that all the elements of *ancien régime* Eton were delineated in their most striking and highly-coloured forms: the fights, the drunkenness, the dissipation, the draconian floggings, the rebellions, the cheek-by-jowl co-existence of the harshest squalor with refined scholarship and vivid intellectual curiosity. In Keate's time the two worlds of the eighteenth century and the Victorian age met each other blindfold. Gladstone was a boy in the school and William Johnson Cory, who was to create a higher, more civilized tradition of education than Eton or any other school had known, entered College at the tender age of nine in 1832. Neither had much to say about Keate but the Eton of their boyhood was the Eton he made famous.

7 *ibid* 44/691.

That Keate should have impressed his image so indelibly on so many minds is one of the curiosities of nineteenth century history. He was conventional to the point of monotony, lacking, so far as can be seen, new ideas of any kind, or even the moral courage to press the minor changes that he wished to make against the blank conservatism of the Provost and Fellows. What he had got, and that in inexhaustible abundance, was pluck. Even the force of personality to which everyone who knew him pays tribute depended on or derived from his exceptional physical courage. For a little man – he was barely five feet tall – to face a mob of five hundred boys most of them bigger and stronger, unused to discipline, often inflamed by drink and egged on to insolence by the yells and catcalls of their fellows, called for a fortitude that compelled the admiration of the young savages who screwed up the doors of his desk or primed his candle-snuffers with gunpowder. He had succeeded a man who had evaded unpleasantness with a smiling irresponsibility. Keate knew he had to take a grip and knew only one way of doing it. Perhaps there was no other. Certainly he caught the imagination of the boys who passed through the school in his time as only a few headmasters in the history of English education have done, a feat the more extraordinary because he seems to have possessed none of this quality himself. To an unusual degree he personified the sovereign virtue of his age, admired and needed then above all others, the bulldog courage that never counts the odds or considers the possibility of giving in. When Keate became Head Master of Eton the country had been at war, with one short interval of eighteen months, since the oldest boy in the school could remember. Alliance after alliance had crumbled: defeat had followed defeat: Napoleon was a military genius: the French army was invincible. No wonder that the Etonians serving in the army of occupation in Paris in 1815 should fête their old Head Master, then on a private visit, as if he had led them to victory. Complete, transparent fearlessness is a rare thing. Keate exemplified it.

And yet what a dull, unadventurous, unattractive place Eton was under him. The incessant floggings by means of which he governed the ungovernable became the one great fact of life.

The birch and the block loomed large in the image of Eton as though it were some kind of penal establishment. But even this ferocious system seems to have left much of the most necessary aspects of discipline in a deplorably lax state. Bullying was too common to excite comment or apology. Fighting was, as we have seen, openly approved by authority. Drunkenness though frowned on and sometimes severely punished was evidently not thought to be a serious or shocking reflection on the school. And what of the masters and of Keate's superintendence of them?

One of the rival candidates for the headmastership when Keate was appointed was a handsome and popular housemaster called Drury. Winthrop Mackworth Praed was in his house and has rhymed his name into one of the lilting, nostalgic verses that have been so often anthologised. In prose memoirs of the time Drury is a conspicuous figure, an elegant scholar, a fine athlete, a man of fashion. Prodigal and reckless, he eventually fled the country leaving a wife and children and £20,000 of debt. Keate had only too good reason to know what was his course of life. A year before he absconded the Head Master's sister-in-law noted in her journal for the autumn half: 'Drury has never been in school since it opened. He has a lame leg, he says; Mr Keate read me such a letter which he had written to him – no one but such a man as Drury would put up with being so taken to task, both for failure in duty and payment to Mr Keate. He now owes him more than £500, which he has over and over again promised to pay.'[8] Drury was then a master of eighteen years standing. That his instability was not merely financial is apparent from Gronow's reminiscences. Drury and another master 'used to start for London after school, to get in time for the theatre, & passed their nights in jovial suppers with that great but eccentric genius, Edmund Kean. They terminated these little expeditions by driving back with very bad headaches (for Edmund always "forswore thin potations") ... One fine day, these jovial pedagogues ... took with them two of my chums, John Scott, the son of Lord Eldon [then Lord

8 *ibid* 53/40, 80/468.

Chancellor] and Lord Sunderland ... the curricles were again brought into play, and they arrived in a few hours at the Hummums, a famous hotel in Covent Garden, where Kean had ordered dinner. With such an example as the great actor, it is no wonder that they drank pretty freely: and as everyone did in those jovial days, they sallied out after dinner in search of adventures. They created such a disturbance that, after several encounters with the watchmen they were taken to Bow Street, & had to be bailed out ... by the secretary of the all-powerful Chancellor. This incident created much scandal. The two tutors were threatened with the loss of their places, and clerical degradation; but Lord Eldon, who was no enemy to a bottle of port, threw over them the mantle of his protection, and they got off without incurring the punishment they so richly deserved.'[9] Drury was by no means the only instance of a scandalous and irregular life among the masters of his time. In the very year that he was appointed, Dr Langford, one of the Fellows who had previously been Lower Master, took refuge from his creditors within the rules of Holyrood (the Edinburgh equivalent of the Fleet as a legal haven for debtors) where he appears to have continued to draw his emoluments for the remaining ten years of his life, notwithstanding the involuntary non-residence that, under the statutes, should have disqualified him.[10]

The discipline that Keate set such store by seems to have been a strange and partial concept. Was it anything more than a self-justifying rationalisation of Eton as it then existed? Dr Langford was by many years senior to Keate but the system that had produced them both was that to which Keate uncritically adhered. His handling of Drury supports this. How can he have thought that so unstable and simply disreputable a figure was fit to be in charge of boys, particularly of boys who were only too likely to slip into the same course of life and were only too easily open to the charm and glamour that Drury had to offer? After eighteen years a strong letter seems an inadequate

9 quot. *Etoniana* 43–4.
10 *ibid* 71/321.

response from so redoubtable a disciplinarian. That it was so the scandal of Drury's absconding amply proved.

The paradox of Keate is that so outstandingly courageous a man should be so intellectually and morally timid. This is ludicrously exemplified in his attitude towards the famous festivities with which the school celebrated George III's birthday, the Fourth of June. The proceedings culminated in a firework display preceded by a procession of boats whose crews magnificently attired in fancy dress were generally far from sober. The school authorities had not adopted the festival and evaded any responsibility for it. On the other hand they did not wish to incur the odium of forbidding so fashionable an occasion, particularly one that fostered Eton's special relationship with the monarchy. The logical result of such feebleness was the pretence of official ignorance. 'I wonder why Mrs Goodall always dines early on the Fourth of June and orders her carriage at six' said the Provost who had been Keate's predecessor as Head Master. Keate resolutely maintained the same fiction, even in 1831 going so far as to refuse an invitation to accompany the King, William IV, to watch the procession of boats on the grounds that 'he did not know there was such a thing'.[11] The atrocities that took place nightly in Long Chamber after he and his butler had locked the door must have been known to him since he had himself been a Colleger. Did he tacitly approve their hardening, toughening effect? Or was he too timid to tamper with the crazy old structure that afforded him so comfortable a lodging?

So far it might be judged that Keate's Eton was a deeply uncivilized place. Yet there were boys in the school whose reading and taste show cultivation as wide as that of any succeeding generation. The journal kept by Lord Metcalfe during his last year at Eton – he was then a boy of 15 and the year was 1800 – shows him reading Voltaire's *Louis XIV* and *Charles XII* and improving his own translation of Rousseau, reading and translating a number of classical authors, Horace, Lucan, Cicero, apparently in his own time as well as studying Homer

11 Maxwell-Lyte, 418–9.

and Virgil in school. He read Ariosto and, among modern authors, Gibbon's occasional writings and Goldsmith's *Deserted Village*. He read the *Rowley Poems*, Chatterton's celebrated forgery, and interested himself in the controversy as to their authenticity, finding himself, as he is honest enough to confess, convinced by each successive argument. He corresponded with the editors of the *Naval Chronicle* and the *Military Journal* and apparently submitted contributions. What is especially striking about his culture is its genuineness and its lack of provincialism. What did such a boy think of Eton? He thought it the best of schools, in the last analysis because it offered the most freedom, though this, he admitted, might be carried too far. 'I have witnessed it at Eton.' Nonetheless 'From study to relaxation, from relaxation to study, is a delightful transition; in the other way of education one trudges on in the usual method of teasing application, and when study no longer becomes a merit it loses *all* its pleasures.'[12]

Another boy's journal, written in 1822 – 3, shows its author already a considerable bibliophile. He gives an enthusiastic and knowledgeable account of the treasures to be found in the library of the Penn family at Stoke Poges and, during the holidays, after being shown round the library at the British Museum, settles down to read there for the rest of the day. When the museum closes he visits the bookshops and records his purchases. Apart from the classics he reads Italian and French, both of which he is taught at Eton outside the regular curriculum. He is an active member of a debating society that applies itself to such questions as whether Napoleon was rightly exiled to St Helena or whether Charles I deserved to be decapitated. It is true that only one member took Napoleon's part and no one could be found to condone regicide but then it was a very small society, consisting of only ten members.[13] Its controversial level was hardly to be compared with the debates of the Eton Society in which Gladstone delivered, with some trepidation, his first public speech on October 29th 1825. The subject was the education of

12 *Etoniana* 91/646 – 8.
13 *ibid*, 51, 1 – 6, Journal of C.P. Golightly.

the poor and both matter and manner gave an ample foretaste of what political audiences were in for for the next seventy years.[14]

Gladstone and his circle prefigure Eton's age of inspiration and intellectual excitement. Arthur Hallam, the son of the Whig constitutional historian, George Selwyn, the future Bishop of New Zealand and Milnes Gaskell, whom all of them except himself thought the most gifted, were its brightest stars. Most of them arrived at the school with a love of literature and all were used to hearing politics talked about by people who took an active part in them. So precocious was Milnes Gaskell's political consciousness that one of his school-fellows said that his nurse must have lulled him to sleep by Parliamentary reports, and his first cries on waking in his cradle must have been 'hear, hear'.[15] Yet there is none of the suffocation, none of the narrowness and aridity so characteristic of the zealot, particularly the immature zealot. They read widely, they argued passionately, but enjoyment and liveliness flash from their letters and journals. Their tastes and pleasures were by no means uniform and they had no wish to make them so. Gladstone enjoyed games but Hallam did not. Gladstone, robust and combative, reports with enthusiasm in his early letters home on the fights that then formed so approved a part of an Eton education. Milnes Gaskell, delicate and refined, clearly hated his first year or so: he was bullied, persecuted and teased: his room was vandalised, his favourite books spoilt, his clothes torn: he objected strongly to the foul language and unpleasant habits that his house tutor seems to have permitted. At last his parents took him away for six months on medical advice and sent him to Brighton. On his return he was, to his infinite relief, sent to live in lodgings with a private tutor. At once the tone changes: everything that he had enjoyed about Eton, its freedom, its sociability, its ambitious standards of scholarship, comes out from behind the clouds: the bullying and the squalor drop away. 'Why do you not congratulate me on the Elysian state of

14 Morley, *Gladstone* i, 35.
15 *ibid*, 39.

happiness that I in common with most other Etonians enjoy?'
he writes to his mother on June 5th 1826.

The letters of these boys, high-spirited and agreeably
frivolous as they often are, seem much more grown-up, much
less provincial, than the preoccupations of the Head Master and
the Governing Body. Keate and Goodall were reckoned
finished scholars by the standards of their day. But what had
they done with their faculties since, as young men, they had
made the approved circuit of the Greek and Latin authors and
had acquired the facility of composing in the metres and the
idiom of the ancients? When the Prince and Princess of Den-
mark visited the school in 1822 none of the three Fellows in
residence could speak a word of French.[16] The incuriosity about
the world they were living in could hardly find a more eloquent,
if mute, expression. By contrast the members of the Eton Society* were looking out at the world and taking in what they saw.
The connexion with the world of affairs that had grown
throughout the eighteenth century was eagerly developed. Canning, as Foreign Secretary, was fond of visiting Eton where he
had a son in the school, and enjoyed talking about politics to
these young enthusiasts. 'What, Gaskell, are you employing
yourself in tracing very accurately the progress of the Elections?
You can't do better.' But he could, for the very next year he was
invited to dine and sleep at the nearby hotel where Canning was
staying and next morning ' ...I had the honor of writing a
dispatch for him to Lord Granville and to Mr Gordon. The one
to Mr Gordon related to what Mr Canning termed "*the intoler-
able pretensions of Brazil*." '[17] Short of an invitation to attend a
Cabinet meeting a higher state of ecstasy was unimaginable. All
this went hand in hand with reading Clarendon and Gibbon,
with construing Homer and Pindar and Virgil and Cicero, with
learning to compose in Latin and Greek. Gladstone and his
friends did not think themselves above what Eton had to offer.
But they did not circumscribe their minds to its limitations.

16 *Etoniana* 79/455.
 * see p. 147.
17 *ibid* 65/238.

Nowhere was this more conspicuous than in the matter of religion. Milnes Gaskell had been shocked by the lack of reverence in chapel. Almost every memoir bears witness to the contemptible quality of the sermons preached by the Fellows, who were generally either inaudible or absurd. No attempt was made to instruct the boys in the teachings of Christianity or to edify them by well ordered acts of worship. To avert rowdyism or at least to preserve a semblance of decency seems to have been the highest aim. By contrast Gladstone and his fellow members took their own religion seriously and tried to understand that of others. Hallam fluttered the dovecotes by making a speech in praise of Mahomet. And of course they, unlike their clerical seniors, were in favour of Catholic Emancipation.

It is characteristic of religious life at Eton in Keate's time that when a great nobleman, the Duke of Newcastle, outlined his plans for founding a scholarship to enrich it his first proposals should be for an examination in the Thirty-Nine Articles. On the basis of this he wished to call it 'The Christian Scholarship'. What the Duke's idea of Christianity was may be gauged from his defending his eviction of tenants who were not of his own political persuasion by quoting in a speech in the House of Lords the text 'Is it not lawful for me to do what I please (*sic*) with mine own?' Fortunately Keate and Goodall induced him to modify the scheme so as to make it principally a test of classical scholarship. But the Duke was sincerely concerned to retain its Christian substructure. For more than a century after its foundation in 1829 the scholarship required a familiarity with the New Testament in Greek and a good general knowledge of the Bible as well as the more traditionally Etonian aptitudes for Latin elegiacs and similar exercises. Gladstone had left Eton and was an undergraduate at Christ Church when the Duke's benefaction was made public. He expressed unqualified delight and eleven years later, in 1840, he was one of the two examiners. This was not his only connexion with the Duke who had brought him into Parliament for his pocket borough of Newark in 1832 and was to turn him out for supporting Peel over free trade in corn in 1846.

Gladstone's life was so long, his devotion to Eton, through all the vicissitudes of his own political opinions, so undeviating that he seems in some way to embody the transition from the erratic and terrifying school of Keate to the gentlemanly, ordered headmastership of Warre. Gladstone himself said that the best picture of the Eton he had known as a boy was that painted by his great (and non-Etonian) rival in his novel *Coningsby*. If it seems to us incredible that such a place could inspire such affection we must remember that the England in which it was set was a much rougher, harsher, wilder society than any of us have known. All our judgements are relative to our own situation as our ancestors' were before us. And all retrospect is subject to nostalgia. When David Copperfield meets Traddles again only a few years after the hell of Salem House Traddles recalls their schooldays with the words: 'Dear me! Well, those were happy times, weren't they?' Gladstone himself recalled with some wonder the extraordinary enthusiasm of the cheering for Keate at an old Etonian dinner in London some years after he had retired from the headmastership. When at last it subsided, Keate rose to reply but was too moved by his reception to string so much as three words together.

To those who have witnessed such scenes the memory will outlive and at last efface any unpleasant recollection. But the historian, a visitor from outer time, comes on the evidence scattered by first-hand experience and values it in proportion to its proximity to the events described. Keate's sister-in-law, Miss Margaretta Brown, who lived in his house throughout his headmastership, kept a diary. From start to finish there is not a word of criticism of a man whom she saw as kindly, unselfish, overworked and mild in every human relationship. Nonetheless the Eton she depicts is not the easy, sunlit land of happy reminiscence. 'Something *very unpleasant* has happened at Dupuis's' ... 'The Carters have again had a boy die in the house – Pusey *mi*.' 'A sad accident too lately happened – by a boy of the name of Watts trying a gun at Jack Hall's in Brocas Lane ... a most cruel and disgraceful business took place at Levi's [a shop-keeper in the High Street who was the periodic victim of anti-Semitic filthiness] ...'[18] All these entries fall within a period of eighteen months and could easily be multiplied. They are perhaps the more telling because they come from a fit consort for Dr Pangloss who, unlike him, would have thought it otiose to state, let alone to repeat, that all was for the best in the best of all possible worlds. A case can be made for the unregulated, unsupervised course of life in Keate's day on the ground that it gave freedom and fostered independence; a case can be made, Keate often made it, for making boys learn to stand up for themselves in a violent world; but it is difficult to see any defence whatever for the abuse of Henry VI's bounty to fatten the Fellows and starve the Collegers. 'From 1828 to 1830, after I was in College, I knew nothing of what went on except that I was starved and flogged, beaten and dirty'[19] wrote Archdeacon Essington, no weakling for he ended his Eton career as Captain of Football. His testimony is so amply confirmed as to make repetition tedious.

Fortunately help was at hand. In 1840 Francis Hodgson was elected Provost after Goodall's reign of thirty years. As the carriage that brought him down from Derbyshire to take up his appointment came through the playing fields and he saw again the buildings in which he had spent five years as a Colleger, his first words were: 'Please God I will do something for those poor boys.' His prayer was answered. College at Eton changed in his time from ugly duckling to swan.

But even earlier Keate must be credited with two appointments to the staff that were to change the whole spirit of the place, much for the better. The first, Edward Coleridge, became his son-in-law: the second Edward Hawtrey, became, in 1834, his successor. 'It was entirely due to Hawtrey' wrote Gladstone in a fragment of recollection 'that I first owed the reception of a spark, the *divinae particulam aurae*, and conceived a dim idea that in some time, manner and degree, I might come to know.'[20] Eton had once again at her head a man of real liberality of mind.

---

18 *ibid* 85/557, 86/570, 571.
19 *ibid* 115/232.
20 Morley, *Gladstone* i, 30.

Perhaps nothing symbolizes the change more neatly than his attitude towards the festivities of the Fourth of June. Keate, it will be remembered, had pretended to know nothing about them. Hawtrey not only acknowledged their existence and thus brought them within the bounds of discipline and order. He made them the central feature of the school's social calendar, ultimately replacing *Montem*, an inexplicable and most undesirable customary feast financed by cadging money from fashionable visitors. To the Fourth of June celebrations in 1843 Hawtrey invited Macaulay, Connop Thirlwall, Bishop of St David's and Panizzi, the great Director of the British Museum.[21] On any showing they were three of the best minds in England and none of them could be reckoned a sound, or even an unsound, Tory. Eton was no longer content to slumber away her time on the down of plenty.

21 *Etoniana* 97/745.

CHAPTER FOUR

———————◦∞◦———————

Victorian Renaissance:
the age of William Johnson Cory

ROUND THE FIRST FLOOR of the cloisters at Eton runs a corridor
that enables those with houses or offices there to visit each other
or to enter the hall or College Library without going outside.
In the nineteen-twenties and thirties when M.R. James was
Provost and Cyril Alington was Head Master both were often
seen there after breakfast comparing their success with *The
Times* crossword puzzle. A century earlier at about five o'clock
in the morning two of the Fellows were pacing anxiously along
the blue carpet which then as now gives the corridor its name.
They had been up all night waiting for a messenger to bring
them the result of the Third Reading of the Great Reform Bill.
As dawn was breaking they heard that the Bill had been carried.
One of them turned to the other with the words, 'This is the
greatest crime since the Crucifixion.' Both men were necessarily
in priest's orders so that no mere blasphemy was intended.

The old gentlemen had already had their first brush with the
forces of reform. In 1818 Brougham as Chairman of a Parliamentary Committee for enquiring into the education of the
lower orders had had the impertinence to cite the ancient
colleges of Winchester and Eton, charged as they were with the
duty of educating poor scholars, to give evidence as to how they
fulfilled their statutory obligations. Loud were the cries of
outraged dignity. Lower orders indeed! The Winchester
authorities tried to evade the summons on the grounds that
their statutes specifically enjoined secrecy, a defence not open
to Eton through the carelessness of an earlier Governing Body
in allowing a master to make a copy of the statutes which had

in the course of time found its way into the British Museum. Both Colleges had in the end to submit to Brougham's examination and Eton did not come at all well out of it. Provost Goodall, asked why the Head Master charged fees to Oppidans and even to Collegers which the statutes explicitly forbade, shuffled and equivocated. His replies when questioned about the wealth of the Fellows and the misery of the scholars were equally unsatisfactory. He had the effrontery to take credit for the provision of vegetables not specified by the Founder at a cost of £100 a year and, a rare luxury no doubt in a fifteenth century school, of knives and of plates. The evidence spoke for itself. Brougham in his report wisely left it to do so, contenting himself with a polite suggestion that the College should itself correct the irregularities that had been exposed. The hint was not taken.

Nonetheless the appointment of Hodgson as Provost and Hawtrey as Head Master meant much more than reform: it meant transformation. Hodgson initiated the long overdue re-housing of the Collegers. The New Buildings were begun in 1844. Of the £14,000 raised by the time the Prince Consort laid the foundation stone the College in its corporate capacity felt able to contribute only £2,000 but the Provost, Head Master and Fellows as private persons subscribed rather more. The change in style of life was matched by a change in method of entry. In 1844, as mentioned earlier, four scholarship candidates were rejected. In 1846 Rowland Williams, the little boy who had been scalped when tossed in a blanket in Long Chamber, was one of the Fellows of King's appointed as examiners. He records his success in making selection *according to merit* (his italics) of twenty out of the fifty-four candidates offering themselves for five vacancies in College.[1] A scholarship at Eton had become a distinction to compete for, not (as heretofore) a nominated meal-ticket to mediocrity. Since for some time yet it was to be either the sole or the main source from which the masters were chosen the difference in quality would make itself felt in the school at large.

1 *Etoniana* 63/196 – 7, 65/228.

Hawtrey as Head Master made some sensible if limited changes in the teaching and administrative arrangements. But the inestimable benefit that he conferred on the school was his talent for appointing interesting and original men to the staff and for supporting them by his loyalty and his sympathy. From his time dates the remarkable succession of masters whose independence of outlook and originality of taste have given Eton its peculiar distinction. Edward Coleridge, William Johnson Cory, Oscar Browning, A.C. Ainger, Francis Warre Cornish, H.E. Luxmoore, A.C. Benson – the list could be prolonged to the period of the nineteen twenties and thirties. These were men of uncommon quality, most of them of high literary sensibility and a number of them successful authors. Hawtrey had ceased to be Head Master before the greater part of them were appointed but in a continuous entity like a school it is the grafting of the new scion on to the old stock that is truly creative. Coleridge, like Hawtrey himself, was Keate's appointment: but it was under Hawtrey that Coleridge spread his wings. His high churchmanship was alarming to the somnolent conventionality of church life at Eton. Ultimately it was to prevent him from succeeding to the headmastership since Queen Victoria's prejudices on the subject were violent even by her own standards. Coleridge also gave offence by the care and professionalism with which he undertook his tutorial duties. In the first twenty-five years of the Newcastle scholarship eleven of the winners were his pupils. Many of them went on to carry off the highest distinctions at Oxford and Cambridge. One such, T.W. Allies, who won the Newcastle in the year it was founded and went on to become a Fellow of Wadham, returned in 1838 to help Coleridge prepare three or four of his most promising boys for the examination. The other masters were outraged. A unanimous letter was sent to their over-zealous colleague, apparently demanding the disqualification of the candidates who had had the advantage of this special coaching. Hawtrey calmed them down but stood by his gifted and energetic subordinate.[2]

Coleridge's annotated list of pupils, from his coming to Eton

2 *ibid* 95/714.

as a master in 1825 to his election to a Fellowship in 1857, shows within a brief compass the range of Eton's contribution to the Victorian age.[3] Perhaps only one other master in his time, William Johnson Cory, could have produced such a record of Cabinet ministers and double firsts. One is struck by the number of early deaths. Travel was more dangerous, even in Europe: one young man drowned in the Jura, another murdered near Marathon. The empire took its toll: 'killed in a cavalry charge at Ferozepoore'; 'killed accidentally in Canada'; 'killed at the Siege of Mooltan, while watching the storm through a narrow slit in a wall'; 'killed at Moodkee'. But a large number survived to perform distinguished service in the colonies as soldiers, judges and administrators. Squires and clergymen are thick on the ground, though perhaps less thick than they had been. The nineteenth century offered so many more options. And Coleridge's high church convictions perhaps played their part in disposing so many of his ablest pupils to follow Newman into the Church of Rome. There were, as might be expected, a number who went into the Household Cavalry and did nothing much, except for two who ruined themselves by gambling and another who wrote the definitive treatise on the Horse's Foot. What is common to all these thumbnail sketches of a career is the note of affection, of gentleness, of concern in the mind of their old tutor. The relationship between teacher and taught had changed.

No one did more to transform it than William Johnson Cory. Appointed by Hawtrey in 1845 and dismissed by Hornby in 1872 in circumstances that have been loudly hushed up, Cory in his life and in his writings gives the most lucid, the most articulate expression to the ideas and standards for which, rightly or wrongly, Eton has been admired. He made the first serious attempt to define its distinction and thus to teach it what it could do. In his universality as in his limitations, in his scepticism as in his ardour he epitomises the idea he served. Just as General de Gaulle's idea of France comprehended Joan of Arc and Voltaire, so Cory was both visionary and iconoclast, poet

3 *ibid* 83/513 – 7, 84/529 – 33, 85/545 – 50.

and critic, modernist and traditionalist, in his approach to Eton. These are whirling words. Some more precise meaning must be winched down to the reader. Who and what was Cory? What did he say? What did he do?

Cory, or rather William Johnson as he was called until, comparatively late in life, he succumbed to the family passion for changing surnames, was born in 1823 and brought up near the small but beautiful property he later inherited in North Devon. At the tender age of nine he was elected to a scholarship at Eton and entered on the delights of stinking mutton, unchecked bullying and insanitary discomfort so feelingly recorded by his contemporaries in Long Chamber. 'As a young boy he won an Eton scholarship' wrote his biographer, and perhaps favourite pupil, Lord Esher.[4] His intellectual brilliance as his subsequent record shows would have carried him to success in any competitive examination. But as we know, and as Cory himself pointed out in his evidence to the Royal Commission on the Public Schools, such was not the method of entry to College when he was a boy. Those early and surely miserable years are passed over in silence by himself, by his biographer and by the editor of his *Letters and Journals*. His first surviving letter, written at the age of fifteen, in the clear, vivacious, elegant prose style that makes dullness impossible, shows him enjoying rowing and acting, reading avidly and with enjoyment a range of classical authors as well as the young Dickens (a taste he was later to deplore). He was an outstanding classical scholar, winning the Newcastle at Eton in 1841 and the Craven at Cambridge in 1844. His Latin and Greek compositions stand in the first rank. Of his small published collection *Lucretilis* Professor Munro wrote,

'I don't mean to flatter you when I tell you that in my humble judgment they are the best and most Horatian Sapphics and Alcaics which I am acquainted with that have been written since Horace ceased to write.'[5] In 1843 he had been Chancellor's Medallist for English poetry. In 1845 he had written, though

4 Esher, *Ionicus* (1923), 14.
5 L[etters] & J[ournals], 567.

not published, his famous translation of Callimachus's beautiful epigram on the death of Heraclitus and his much-anthologised poem Mimnermus in Church, the one for his earliest pupils at Eton and the other composed on the terrace of the Star and Garter at Richmond while waiting for his first dinner as a member of the Apostles, the Cambridge club that traditionally disdains conventional opinions and ordinary abilities. It expresses his view of life better than anyone else can, so perhaps it may be convenient to reprint it here:

> You promise heavens free from strife,
>   Pure truth, and perfect change of will;
> But sweet, sweet is this human life,
>   So sweet, I fain would breathe it still;
> Your chilly stars I can forego,
>   This warm kind world is all I know.
>
> You say there is no substance here,
>   One great reality above:
> Back from that void I shrink in fear,
>   And child-like hide myself in love:
> Show me what angels feel. Till then,
>   I cling, a mere weak man, to men.
>
> You bid me lift my mean desires
>   From faltering lips and fitful veins
> To sexless souls, ideal quires,
>   Unwearied voices, wordless strains:
> My mind with fonder welcome owns
>   One dear dead friend's remembered tones.
>
> Forsooth the present we must give
>   To that which cannot pass away;
> All beauteous things for which we live
>   By laws of time and space decay.
> But oh, the very reason why
>   I clasp them, is because they die.

Cory's intellectual sympathies were not overwhelmed by his love of ancient literature or by his ear for verse. At Cambridge

he had come under the influence of the Anglo-Catholic revival
so eloquently expounded at Oxford by Newman and his friends:
but he felt also, and even more strongly, the force of the moral
and philosophical arguments of Bentham and James Mill. The
effect of these powerful cross-currents was not to make him
strike out for the shore but to adventure more boldly and to
extend the bounds of his curiosity. He read widely in French
and German literature: he became, and remained, a historian: he
interested himself in economics (both these subjects were then
virtually unrecognised in the courses of study offered by the
universities) and he developed a passion for politics. Above all
he was a man of his time, no mere wistful antiquarian occasionally peering with puzzled or alarmed distaste at the world outside his college windows. 'Our own times are altogether the
best.'[6] He once said that all a boy needed was to be able to read
that morning's *Times* intelligently.[7] He had originally intended
to read for the Chancery Bar and was entering himself at an Inn
when in March 1845 Hawtrey invited him, at short notice, to
join the staff at Eton. Six weeks earlier he had written to a friend
about the possibility: 'If I go there I am quite bound to make
endeavours as a reformer; my convictions as to the alterations
desirable there being very positive, very strong, and pretty well
known ... I can hardly think I could [act upon them], and if I
could not I should be in a very false position. And I think there
are heavy temptations for an Eton master towards love of
money, gormandizing, jealousy, intrigue and imposture. And
yet I should like to be forming an ingenuous mind instead of
blackening a mischievous parchment. Pupils might give a man
more happiness than clients. But the truth is I distrust the purity
of the motives which have this long time past swayed me
towards a wish to be an Eton master.'[8] Is this an oblique
allusion to the sexual overdrive that was to intensify, sometimes
unbearably, the affectionate and admiring attachments he formed with his pupils? It might equally emanate from the strong,

6 *Ionicus*, 32.
7 T.L.S. 2 June 1950.
8 L & J 28.

and still specifically Christian, consciousness of talents to be accounted for that his letters and journals continue to display at this time and for several years after.

The tension between the teachings of Christianity and the morality to be extracted from the Greek and Roman poets and philosophers gave a peculiar tang to the education in schools and colleges such as Eton that had no alternative to believing the one or to teaching the other. Cory's poem 'Mimnermus in Church' states the dilemma and boldly accepts the pagan view. But a poet and a teacher must speak with many voices, assume different identities, enter into many minds. Cory's mind was open to every argument that he judged coherent, not simply to what he read in school or heard in church. Most of all, since he had a far wider range of reading than most dons or schoolmasters of his day, he was open to the ideas of his contemporaries. Reading John Stuart Mill's *Autobiography* on its publication in 1873, when he was no longer an Eton master, he wrote: 'The book has roused me a good deal and I could write reams about it. It takes me back to the winter of 1846, when I sent out to the shop for the Logic, then nearly a new book and a heavy expense for me, and I read it right off with a sense of mental expansion never felt before or since.' He had called Mill 'my old *master*' and he went on, 'There are three other teachers of my youth to whom I am still apt to turn: Wordsworth, Newman and Ruskin.'[9] Whatever may be thought of Cory's ideas they were not narrow. And there is no mistaking, in anything he wrote, the thrill of intellectual excitement.

It was this that made him such an incomparable teacher, certainly the greatest in the history of Eton. Herbert Paul, an academic of a much cooler, drier temper who had been his pupil, wrote 'He was in a class by himself, differing not in degree but in kind from all the other teachers that I, at least, have ever known ... Nothing that he taught could ever for a moment, while he taught it, be dull. He never seemed as if he tried to be interesting, but as if he could not be anything else. That he was teaching "dead languages" never occurred either to

9 *Ionicus*, 56.

him or to his pupils. It was the living voice that came to us.' And one of the pupils of his old age has spoken of 'Cory's miraculous power of teaching twenty things at once, so that you were in the midst of the French Revolution or the law about English juries when you thought you were learning the First Aorist or mastering some dates in Greek history.'[10] Part of his fascination lay in the singularity of his opinions. Like the ever-memorable John Hales he disconcerted his literary and scholarly friends by the high place he accorded to contemporary writers. Few then, and fewer now, could share his view that Tennyson was a greater poet than Milton or that Sardou was a finer dramatist than Shakespeare or Aeschylus. But such judgments, whatever one might think of them, were not flippant or lazy. The lounging brilliance that self-flattering Etonians like to assume as their characteristic posture was not favoured by Cory. He was extremely industrious. Eleven hours hard reading might go to the preparation of a lecture, probably never repeated, on some subject that his vigilant intelligence had perceived on the far periphery of what he happened to be teaching. He steadfastly disapproved of his admiring ex-pupil and colleague Oscar Browning, who had much of his old tutor's brilliance and charm, on the grounds that he did not exert himself. 'I will be quite open with you,' Cory wrote in 1869, 'I should not have recommended any boy to you if he was meant to be a scholar. I perceived very soon after you came here that, as I have told you before, you did not throw yourself into what I call the school work.'[11]

What Cory conceived the function of a school to be he has defined in prose, limpid, graceful, succinct, such as all too few writers on educational topics can command:

'You go to school at the age of twelve or thirteen; and for the next four or five years you are not engaged so much in acquiring knowledge as in making mental efforts under criticism. A certain amount of knowledge you can indeed with average faculties acquire so as to retain; nor need you regret the hours

10 T.L.S. 2 June 1950.
11 Wortham, *Oscar Browning*, 70 – 1.

that you spent on much that is forgotten, for the shadow of lost knowledge at least protects you from many illusions. But you go to a great school, not for knowledge so much as for arts and habits; for the habit of attention, for the art of expression, for the art of assuming at a moment's notice a new intellectual posture, for the art of entering quickly into another person's thoughts, for the habit of submitting to censure and refutation, for the art of indicating assent or dissent in graduated terms, for the habit of regarding minute points of accuracy, for the habit of working out what is possible in a given time, for taste, for discrimination, for mental courage and mental soberness. Above all, you go to a great school for self-knowledge.'

What would Dr Keate have made of this? It was, surely, reaction to Keate's Eton that made Cory a radical and a rationalist as it made him a romantic. He was, from the beginning, as deeply aware of the limitations of the place as he was of its potentialities. 'It is this systematic talk with a well-educated reasoner which I am always wishing for ... A schoolmaster must needs get dogmatic or weak in faith or both unless he has some such intercourse with equals or superiors – & it is of infinite importance that they be men of his own age,'[12] he wrote after he had been a master for little over a year. After twenty the need had not lessened: 'Cambridge is the place where men, holding perhaps strong opinions, can coolly compare notes, and help each other to understand a question without arguing ... Woe's me, that I must live where no such men dwell ...'[13] Cory's fineness of perception and his power to awaken this quality in his pupils were sustained by the tensions of his mind and of his taste: between the classical and the modern, between the need for maturity and the love of youth, between radical opinions and aristocratic prejudices, between reverence and scepticism. He was as fierce an opponent and critic of comfortable bourgeois selfishness and of the ideas that derived from it as Marx, but it was to the individual not to the aggregate that he responded.

12 L & J, 46.
13 *ibid*, 154.

Yet his mind penetrated to the facts and tendencies underlying his age with a directness that must disconcert those who would write him off as a mawkish archetype of Mr Chips, a nostalgic homosexual sentimentalist. Since the 1920s it has become a commonplace of the history books to date the decline of British power from the late nineteenth century when both Germany and America were overtaking our output of coal and steel. But how many observers recognised this at the time or grasped its significance? Cory did. 'Two things oppress me,' he wrote to his old pupil, the future Lord Esher, in 1872 '(1) *iron* is getting so dear that the Yanks are soon to undersell us and we have opened the chapter of decline as the coal pits are failing. (2) The art of destruction is the most prosperous of all arts and we are throwing our precious steel into the sea instead of piercing the mountains with it.'[14] Lord Palmerston had shewn good judgment in putting forward Cory's name for the Regius Professorship of History at Cambridge in 1860.

It was the universality, the openness, of Cory's mind that made his influence on Eton so enriching. A man of letters himself he was not deluded by prejudice or self-love into the belief that a literary education is a sufficient mental equipment for modern life. Discussing what we now, thanks to Charles Snow, call the Two Cultures, in the England of his youth he wrote: 'As in a Mahometan country despots and their servile delegates accept with a sort of condescension a machine or a mode of locomotion, and treat the foreigner who introduces it as one that is perhaps just a little above a hired juggler or dancing girl, so did the men of letters and the wordmongers of professional life deign to applaud Sir Humphry Davy the discoverer of new metals, or Sir Charles Bell the anatomist of nerves, not dreaming of any philosophy that should indicate a necessary connection between the fixed humanities and the moving sciences.'[15]

Trying to sum up what he had been endeavouring to do in his life's work, Cory quoted two axioms that he said had guided

14 *Ionicus*, 54.
15 Cory, A G[uide] to M[odern] E[nglish] H[istory], i, (1880), 123.

him. ' "Every school should make the most of that which is its characteristic. Eton should continue to cultivate taste." Someone else of equal authority has said "It is greatly to be lamented that for so many years of early life the reasoning faculties should be almost entirely neglected" ... after twenty years of petty toil I am sometimes tempted to imagine that I know how to combine the cultivation of taste with the cultivation of the reasoning faculties.'[16]

It is characteristic of his candour that he admits to a strong partiality for the aristocracy that has historically formed so important an element in Eton. 'I have become a Republican;' he wrote in 1874, 'but ... I find room in a republic for nobles; and I continue to be a backer of Aristocracy. The two notions are compatible. "Honour all men" is the foundation of high republican policy. Thus in France every man is Monsieur, every man expects to be treated with grave respect; not with that mocking courtesy which is in fashion in England, that courtesy of the rich and the great ... An aristocracy which gives men like Dufferin, Northbrook, Carnarvon a fair chance of getting to the front early, before generosity and sweetness dry up, is a great blessing, provided always there be no artificial barrier set up against men of less good birth.'[17] To avow such opinions is to expose oneself to the charge of being a toady and a snob. There is not the slightest evidence that anyone who knew Cory thought him one. His freethinking challenge to all the orthodoxies of discipline, of teaching and, by implication, of religion made him enemies enough to bring out anything that would have told against him. Hornby, the Head Master in 1872, did not disguise his satisfaction in being able to get rid of him. What Cory perceived in aristocracy in contrast with the other classes of society was what he saw in youth as against the other ages of man. Indeed in the passage just quoted he expressly identifies the two. Like the Greek poet Mimnermus whose name he took for his famous poem he wept for the transience of youth's flowering. To catch its reflection was reward enough for his efforts.

16 L & J, 201.
17 *ibid*, 368 – 9.

> Perhaps there's neither tear nor smile,
>   When once beyond the grave.
> Woe's me: but let me live awhile
>   Amongst the bright and brave

*   *   *

> I'll borrow life and not grow old;
>   And nightingales and trees
> Shall keep me, though the veins be cold,
>   As young as Sophocles
>
> And when I may no longer live,
>   They'll say, who knew the truth,
> He gave whate'er he had to give
>   To freedom and to youth.

What Cory did in the last analysis was not to remodel the curriculum (much though he may have contributed to this by his championing of new subjects and his insistence on the teaching of mathematics) but to set a tone. It was a tone that for all its freshness and intimacy drew the essentials of its character from what was already there. Eton was aristocratic, worldly, metropolitan. These terms could easily be converted into exclusive, cold-hearted, fashionable. It was Cory's aim to idealize and refine them, to purge them of vulgarity, selfishness and triviality and to do so without recourse to the traditional Christianity that the place was committed to uphold but which he could not accept. He stood for the cultivation of sensibility, for the training of the critical faculty, for teaching the art of argument. His originality consisted in seeing that much of what he needed lay ready to hand in the old classical system in which he had himself been brought up. The favourite butt of its opponents was the importance it attached to the composition of Latin verses. Not long before his death Cory, reminiscing on this subject to an old pupil, wrote 'Absurd as the Eton schooling was, it had the one redeeming charm of giving one the curious pleasure of authorship.'[18]

18 *ibid*, 566.

The tyrannical pedantry that sought to confine the classical education to the barrack square of grammar and syntax, to throttle not to awaken literary curiosity, was challenged by Cory and those whom he inspired, either directly as tutor and colleague, as in the case of Oscar Browning, A.C. Ainger or Luxmoore, or by example and precept, as in the case of A.C. Benson and George Lyttelton. Just how mechanical and repulsive classical scholarship could be made even for a clever boy with a natural aptitude for it may be judged from this instance recorded, at sixty years distance from the event, by A.C. Ainger. 'We were construing our Horace with him [a colleague of Cory's], and we all knew the lesson. But there was a reference to Juvenal in Orelli's notes which we had none of us looked out – probably we none of us owned a Juvenal – certainly we were quite unaware of our duty in the matter. He set us all to write out the tenth satire (367 lines) – a simply monstrous penalty for what was really no offence at all.'[19] It is hardly surprising that, faced with this sort of thing, one of the most brilliant of nineteenth-century Etonians, F.W. Maitland, should have carried away from the place a lifelong distaste for the study of Greek and Latin.

Cory's legacy to Eton is at once so obvious and so elusive, taking so many forms and yet remaining so much of a piece, that no attempt at definition is satisfactory. He founded a literary tradition that is not yet extinct. He raised the intellectual spirits of the place. He despised platitudes and taught others to despise them. Perhaps most important of all he established a redoubt of radicalism, of sceptical independence of mind, in an institution generally held to represent the conservative and the conventional in their most approved forms. When, late in life, long after he had left Eton, Cory married and had a son, he christened him Andrew because 'no Monarch or Pope had borne that name'.[20] Yet along with all this he was a romantic Imperialist of the brightest hue, glorying in every success of British arms, sitting in sackcloth and ashes at every reverse. 'Brats, the British

19 A.C. Ainger. *Eton Sixty Years Ago* (1917), 222 – 3.
20 *ibid* 235.

Army' he used to cry, leading the rush from his pupil room, as the distant shrilling and thumping of fife and drum came up from the High Street. Like Sir Walter Scott whom he passionately admired he would have been a soldier if he could. This at any rate was a taste that he shared with a younger colleague, Edmond Warre, who was as Head Master from 1884 to 1905 to exert the other great formative influence on the school in its Victorian heyday.

CHAPTER FIVE

Certainties and Doubts:
the age of Warre and Benson

WHEN CORY WAS SUMMARILY DISMISSED from Eton in 1872 neither he nor anyone else seems to have taken any notice of the financial penalty inflicted. When his old pupil Oscar Browning was dismissed in 1875 loud were the lamentations, reaching their crescendo in a special debate in the House of Commons in April 1876, over the severity of the blow. As an Eton house-master, Browning reckoned that he had enjoyed a disposable income of £3,000. He had lived at a very high rate, travelling about Europe with a personal servant, engaging suites at the best hotels, buying pictures and books without stint, hunting when he felt so inclined and keeping a table that was luxurious to the point of ostentation. All that could be saved from the wreck of his fortunes was his Fellowship at King's, bringing in £300 a year, a spar to which he clung till his death in 1923 even though he spent the last fifteen years of his life in Rome. Cory, more fastidious in these as in other matters, resigned his King's Fellowship after his dismissal.

Cory had been the first classical tutor not to take holy orders. This was, in the Eton of the fifties, to renounce the special privileges and prospects enjoyed by this small body of fifteen or twenty men, who alone had the right of succession to a boarding house (as opposed to a dame's house: see p. 38) and the ultimate expectation of a Fellowship. 'In a school number-ing upward of 700 no young classical master had to wait long for promotion to a house, and, after serving a moderate number of years, he might look forward to a retiring pension, made up of a house in the Cloisters, and a comfortable vicarage in the

South of England, with an income from both sources perhaps amounting to £1,200 a year in cash.'[1] This project took no account of the possibilities of other preferment in the Church. No wonder that a mastership at Eton was regarded as a snug berth for a classical scholar.

The Royal Commission on the Public Schools that reported in 1864 opened this secluded establishment to the public view. The failure of the College authorities to act on the recommendations of Brougham's earlier inquiry left them poorly placed to claim that they had justified their privileges by the conscientious discharge of their trust. This time there was to be no nonsense. An Act of 1868 forced Eton to put forward its own programme of radical change on pain of having one imposed on it by outsiders. The old statutes, clad in the ivy of comfortable sinecures, were pulled down. Fellowships of the old type were abolished in favour of a new unpaid non-residential governing body which would meet several times a year. The old exclusive connexion with King's was broken. In a word the shell of the medieval priestly corporation was stripped off.

What went for the constitution, went for the curriculum. The classics, like the clergymen, lost their virtual monopoly but both were long to exercise at least a formal dominion over the school. The Head Master, Dr Balston, who was in office at the time of the commission and gave evidence before it, felt that its recommendations were so opposed to the opinions he had expressed in his answers that it would best become him to resign. He was succeeded by Hornby, the first Head Master for nearly two centuries to come from Oxford and one of the very few not to have been in College as a boy at Eton. The breach in custom was widened by the appointment of another ex-Oppidan, Edmond Warre, as his successor. Both men though reckoned reformers were of a conservative cast of mind and both, themselves fine athletes, were disposed to encourage games and the simple philistinism attendant on them. In temperament they were far removed: Hornby cool, sceptical, courtly: Warre ardent, tender, headstrong. Both disliked the radicalism, the

1 Ainger. *Eton Sixty Years Ago*, 336.

72

independent critical spirit and the cultivation of the individual and the exceptional for which Cory had won such a following among masters and boys. But whereas Hornby did not conceal his relief, not to say his enthusiasm, in dismissing both Cory and Browning, some of their colleagues thought that had Warre been Head Master neither would have been sent away.

What Warre, the happy, affectionate, uncomplicated rowing blue, had in common with Cory was a romanticism that found its fullest expression in military excitement. Both men were patriots, both steeped in the literature of Greece and Rome, both generous, imaginative, high-spirited and unworldly. They took their ideas of war from the heroic set-pieces of antiquity, not, as we do, from the limitless incomprehensible slaughter of recent experience and future expectation. Both were exuberant, flag-waving Imperialists and brought their vision into prominence at Eton by teaching and example. Warre as an undergraduate at Balliol had found time between rowing for the university and winning both a First in Greats and a Fellowship at All Souls to take the lead in forming the Oxford University Rifle Volunteer Corps.[2] No sooner had he arrived at Eton as a temporary master than he threw himself into the movement for a National Rifle Association to encourage every fit man to qualify himself to fight for his country. The Corps became a sacred duty. It was noticed that he did not allow his ordination as a priest in 1867 to curtail his martial exertions. Three weeks of his Christmas holidays in 1870 were spent in Winchester Barracks attached to the King's Royal Rifle Corps where he obtained a certificate of proficiency. When as commanding officer of the Corps he was made a colonel he was the only man in the Army List to bear the title Reverend. This is not to imply that his religion was superficial. In comparing him to Dr Arnold, his biographer is emphatic: '. . . he steered by the same star . . . and he would have been totally unable to grasp the idea of basing education on anything but an entirely Christian foundation'.[3] With the sharp eyes of a boy Percy Lubbock

2 C.R.L. Fletcher *Edmond Warre* 34 ff.
3 *ibid*, 102.

watched the Head Master's unselfconscious engagement in Wesley's great hymn 'Come, O Thou Traveller Unknown' and was moved by his response to its climax:

> 'Tis Love! 'tis Love! Thou diedst for me!
> I hear thy whisper in my heart.
> The morning breaks, the shadows flee;
> Pure universal Love thou art.[4]

It was the grand, simple humanity of Warre that made itself valued in the Eton of his day, transcending and shaming the cold and the smooth. Sir Lawrence Jones has left an unforgettable glimpse of him on the terrible morning when two boys were burnt to death before the eyes of their friends in spite of desperate attempts to break the barred window behind which they were trapped:

> It was about five o'clock on a flawless summer morning; my tutor's house had just been burnt down; two little boys, both of them my fags, had died in the flames; and the Head Master, who had arrived on the scene in pyjamas and a grey woollen dressing-gown had taken me back with him to the Cloisters, and had put me, shivery and shaken, into his own bed. I saw tears roll down his weather-beaten cheeks as he stood, shaving, by the window; he did not seem to despise me, a boy old enough to be already in the VIII, because I was crying on his pillows.[5]

That he was, for all his conscientiousness and scholarship, an uninspired teacher seems clear. 'Not one of us dreamed of listening seriously to Warre in a school-hour; we waited politely for it to pass.'[6] That he was inept and tactless in his handling of his staff A.C. Benson's scintillating journal provides abundant evidence. And Benson was the man Warre himself wanted as his successor. Benson, touchy, brilliant, sarcastic, everything

---

4 Percy Lubbock *Shades of Eton*, 30 – 2.
5 L.E. Jones *A Victorian Boyhood*, 178. A.C. Benson in his unpublished journal savagely derides what he represents as Warre's lachrymose failure to discharge his responsibilities. See Newsome, *On the Edge of Paradise* (1980), 77 – 8.
6 Lubbock, 14.

indeed that Warre was not, yet found the affectionate simplicity of his nature irresistible, as in this vividly recorded scene. The Head Master had sent for Benson and after shuffling papers on his desk, and giving other signs of embarrassment burst out that 'he had something on his mind to tell me, and had wished to say it for long – he wished me to take Orders ... he could not be Head Master long ... and he hoped that I should succeed him ... He put his hand on my arm as we stood by the fireplace and said, rather confusedly, with his hand over his eyes "I have unburdened my mind of this; I have long thought of this, and thought I ought to speak ... I have not liked speaking ... but I have spoken because I hold you liege (or did he say lief?) and dear." It is at a moment like that that I feel I could do anything for him ...'[7] It says much for Warre's integrity and sense of duty that he should tackle Benson on such a subject: Benson, the son of an archbishop and himself, like Cory, a man of bold and critical intelligence:

> Christ could not have been God: he had nothing to say about the whole fabric of nature which in his capacity as Creator he must have had the moulding of ... Did Christ know the earth went round the sun?[8]

Such reflections, so clear, so sharp, so disturbing, could hardly have presented themselves to Warre. Deploring the small proportion of boys leaving Eton with the intention of taking Orders he commented to a diocesan conference 'No doubt there are intellectual difficulties.' 'But over this point,' (writes his biographer) 'Warre passes lightly. Whether he ever grasped how great those intellectual difficulties have become I have never quite been able to discover – he hated to allude to the subject – trampled it down, as it were.'[9]

Warre's ascendancy, like Keate's, was one of personality, not intellect. Percy Lubbock, a boy in Benson's house, defines his recollection of him: 'Warre, splendid among schoolmasters, was not a schoolmaster at all. He was a leader, a statesman, a

7 A.C. Benson MS journal, 4 May 1901.
8 *ibid* 16 June 1885.
9 Fletcher, 258 – 9.

prime minister, and he loved the ancient state that he governed. He loved Eton, he loved and believed in England – believed in England indeed so profoundly that his highest hope for Eton was that the school should please and satisfy the country.'[10] Generous, large-hearted, magnanimous as all accounts show him to have been Warre's influence asserted the claims of the heart and helped to form the atmosphere of late Victorian and Edwardian Eton. But in one important respect his spirit ran counter to the genius of the place. 'His sympathies' wrote his friend and biographer C.R.L. Fletcher, 'went out most to "average people"; perhaps he had a certain distrust of exceptional brilliance especially if it were not combined with exceptional industry. He hated above all things the spirit of emulation ... it was perhaps a defect in Warre's character that he had too little sympathy for "strange" boys, for what one would now call clever "freaks" ...'[11]

In the fifties Swinburne had been in the same division as Warre. Habitually late for early school, when he appeared with a shock of red unbrushed hair, trailing shoelaces and an avalanche of books slipping from his arm the division master would say, 'Here comes the Rising Sun.'[12] Victorian Eton was good-tempered and gentle compared with the age that had preceded it. The horrors of Long Chamber, the wholesale floggings of Keate, had passed into history. But there was still a good deal of bullying, especially of the smaller, younger Collegers by loutish Oppidans and, in some houses, a great deal too much beating. And the old lawlessness and arrogance did not melt away in a night. Edward Lyttelton, who was to succeed Warre as Head Master in 1905, was a boy in the school from 1868 to 1874. Although in his day fights were becoming rare the almost complete failure to provide games for any except the biggest and most senior boys meant that 'there were very many afternoons when we were reduced to amusing ourselves as best we could, and the form it generally took was to sally forth... provoking fights with wholly unoffending "cads":

10 *op. cit.* 14 – 5.
11 Fletcher, 64 – 5.
12 *ibid* 14.

the name given to all young males in England who had never been to one of the accredited Public Schools.'[13] Drinking, or at any rate drunkenness, was no longer acceptable except on the Fourth of June. 'The first "gentleman" I ever saw drunk was before I was thirteen on June 4th: a big Lower boy with a well-known name, reeling about, a disgusting spectacle.'[14]

In the last quarter of the century the tone of the place became steadily more civilised. Partly this reflected the manners of the society that sent its sons to Eton: partly, on Lyttelton's showing especially, the provision for playing games from the late seventies and eighties removed an obvious cause of trouble. But in his view an even more considerable change was that which took place in the relationship between masters and boys. 'The masters, as a lot, were entirely aloof from the boys ... During the years in question there was no such thing as pastoral care exercised by a master, except by one or two of the very youngest, whose example told most beneficially later on, especially H.E. Luxmoore.'[15] Lyttelton never errs on the side of understatement. When he entered the school Cory and Oscar Browning were senior figures and A.C. Ainger and Warre Cornish were their disciples among the younger men. But Lyttelton, eccentric and impulsive as he was, speaks for generations of Etonians in singling out Luxmoore as one of the great creative figures in the history of the school.

Almost unknown outside Eton Luxmoore absorbed, united and exemplified the vivifying influences of Cory and Warre. Refining them, incorporating them into the old continuity of classical learning and Christian piety he transmitted them through a host of pupils, among them M.R. James, the greatest Provost for three centuries. Like Cory, Luxmoore was not only a fine scholar and a remarkable teacher but a man of fastidious taste and wide intellectual curiosity. An artist, he drew and painted with delicacy and truth. He enriched the chapel and the school with many beautiful things and in the course of his long

13 Lyttelton, *Memories and Hopes*, 21.
14 *ibid* 35.
15 *ibid* 22 – 3.

life at Eton – he returned there as a master in 1864 and lived
on in active retirement till 1926 – he prevented his colleagues
and superiors from the enthusiastic destruction of inherited
beauties to which ancient foundations are so easily moved. His
memorial to succeeding generations of boys and visitors is the
garden he created from which, appropriately, the chapel is best
seen. He wrote little for publication but his letters, like Cory's,
were so expressive and so admirably written that a selection
from them was published soon after his death. The beauty of
his character is transparent, matching that of his person and
reflecting what he perceived in nature, in art, in music, in
literature and in the people with whom he had to do. There
is a touch of St Francis of Assisi about Luxmoore. He challenged vulgarity and selfishness and sluggishness with a force of
mind and an unselfconscious example of life that made him
feared.

Simply as a human bridge spanning the most luminous
period of Eton's history Luxmoore is unique. He was elected
a scholar in 1852, the year of Keate's death, was taught by Cory
(whose colleague he was to become) and was still, in active
retirement, a prominent figure in the days when Aldous Huxley
was teaching and Connolly and Orwell were in College. But
Luxmoore was much more than the Nestor of the early twentieth century. He stimulated the moral and aesthetic impulses of
his pupils, drawing out, as perhaps only a temperamentally shy
and diffident man could, their half-formed tastes and propensities. 'His desire was that you should have a chance of knowing
what was best: and so, if you showed an interest in great poetry
or great buildings or pictures or music or plays, he would lavish
his time and his money on helping you to see and understand
them ... On the other hand, he required of you your best, and
never flinched from telling you when he thought you were slack
in giving it: in conduct as well as in work.'[16] Thus M.R. James,
his old pupil and friend of fifty years. Like Cory he made the
classical education a gate that opened on the whole world of
ideas. To quote from a pamphlet he wrote in 1885:

16 E.C.C. 6/12/26.

The end and aim of the whole classical system is to stir our sympathies for great men and other times, and to develop nobility of feeling by beauty of style. If for the sake of beauty and nobility the literature of Greece and the history of Rome still claim their place in education, surely these can also be won by the influence of this once beautiful place, and by sympathy with the goodly works of our own forefathers or the historic associations of England. To us the ages have bequeathed somewhat of which we are but guardians for our time: the continuity of Eton history and much of the best power of her influence are lost if we abuse that trust.[17]

Luxmoore had been deeply influenced, as had Cory, by Ruskin. But whereas in Cory's case this had been counterpointed by his lifelong admiration for Mill and the Philosophic Radicals Luxmoore's sympathy for Ruskinian ideas was closer and more exclusive. He was more of an artist, less of a thinker; more of a saint, less of a genius. Luxmoore certainly recognised his own limitations, perhaps exaggerated them, and could remember only too well the listlessness and lumpishness of adolescence:

'At Eton from 11 years onward what most impresses me is the same singularly mechanical manner of life which I have already noticed. Here was I, a boy certainly of some taste for art, some literary capacity (for I took 3rd into College) and even I fancy some instinctive liking for goodness yet I cannot remember any intellectual effort or any moral effort – an unconscious automaton was I just taking colour and conduct from my surroundings – a chameleon, good with good boys, naughty with naughty boys, doing lessons or not doing lessons just as it happened ... I passed through his [William Johnson Cory's] division without any recognition of being in contact with a man of real genius. He was to me just like any other except that he very properly had me whipped for prompting a boy in saying lesson [the Eton term for learning by heart].'[18] Yet looking back over his life he wrote: 'At Eton for 40 years I blundered and struggled, felt my way for myself and learned my business by

17 *quot. ibid.*
18 Letters, 258 – 9.

rule of thumb ... 2 things only I w^d note as continuing my education – one the inspiring friendship of Wm Johnson whom I had before so stupidly neglected, and the other some intercourse with John Ruskin and the publication of his later work. Difficult as his social economy was at first to me, the longer I live and the more I see of the development of England the more I wonder at his insight ...'[19]

Both Luxmoore and Cory had the true Socratic quality of knowing how little they knew in relation to what there was to know. Their intellectual curiosity was not idle but passionate. Both were manifestly humble men, claiming nothing for their range of mind and seeking no rewards in academic position or fame, still less in money for their attainments. 'Eton is very like University life, and I got here what I did not there cramped by shyness and by want of means and want of sense too – but no substitute for knowledge can be picked up afterwards. I go on learning here, and get in 3 years what a young man betwen 17 and 24 assimilates in a morning.'[20] Who would think that this was an Eton housemaster of twenty-five years standing writing to a pupil who had just gone up to the university? That Eton was more like a university than any other public school was largely thanks to the spirit infused by these two great teachers, refusing themselves the shelter of the comfortable certainties that they encouraged their pupils to question. Neither accepted the axiomatic scepticism that is in its way as easy and complacent as an axiomatic faith. Both would have been incapable of sneering at or even unsettling the personal convictions of the boys they taught. The central fruitful paradox of Victorian Eton, the preferred school of Cabinet ministers, Imperial administrators, generals, financiers and what not, is that at the heart of it was a concern with the individual that would have well become the hero of an E.M. Forster novel, and a search for truth that led to such sources as Mill and Newman, Ruskin and Walter Scott.

Both men combined their power to encourage and to

19 *ibid*, 262.
20 *ibid*, 36.

stimulate with a severe, exacting scholarship. M.R. James stressed this in the *éloge* on Luxmoore already quoted. And Cory was famous for his power of quelling the dull and the idle 'with a sort of contemptuous neglect'.[21] The keenness of their standards was felt, sometimes uncomfortably, by their colleagues. Cory's reproof to Oscar Browning has been mentioned: but Luxmoore was no more indulgent. 'He [A.C. Benson] went too far (I think) in avoiding difficulty and all that boys dislike, brain sweat & sap [an Etonian expression, of Latin derivation, derisively applied both to diligent study and to those who engage in it] it is easily overdone, but it may be underdone too. You can't train sound hard-headed men on kindergarten methods only & A.C.B. turned out no good scholar from his pupil room I think though he charmed & stimulated boys as he would anyone he met.'[22] The object of this censure had earlier admitted its truth in his journal:

> I have been reading the Cory letters and feel ashamed of myself and my work ... I have a flood of inaccurate knowledge & I suppose a certain sympathy – an intuitive knowledge of what is interesting to an ill-regulated mind like my own – and so in an ordinary lesson I can interest the boys without taking much trouble. I think I inherit a knack of teaching ... My own mind is as inconsequent & wanting in grip and hardness as ever. I have a great interest in literature & style & epigram – but no knowledge of history, no grasp of philosophy – a lot of half-fledged ideas.[23]

So would you have us believe, the reader may inquire, that this concern over gem-cutting intellectual techniques really communicated itself to the great mass of coarse-fibred, high-fed, cricketing, footballing, young philistines briefly domiciled at Eton on their way to the City boardrooms or the Tory benches? Scholarship is for scholars. The boys who sat under these highly trained and highly accomplished performers got in

21 H.S. Salt *Memories of Bygone Eton* (1928), 112 ff gives an interesting account of what is was like to be taught by Cory, the more valuable because the author disapproved of his ideas and of the social system in which Eton was rooted.
22 Luxmoore. *Letters* 124 – 5.
23 MS Journal 9 July 1897.

general no more out of doing so than the bodies of tourists marching through the great galleries of Europe get from the works of art before which they are momentarily halted. What nonsense it all is, this teaching the grammatical minutiae of a dead language to boys who hardly know more than the slovenliest usage of their own. And as for that Etonian *specialité de la maison*, the turning out of Latin verses by pupils who have no ear for metre and no feeling for form, might they not be as well occupied turning prayer-wheels like novices in a lamasery?

There is no denying the force of this criticism. It was stated by a number of Eton masters and boys in the heyday of the system. H.S. Salt who shook the dust of an Eton house from his feet to tricycle off, eyes flashing with vegetarian fervour, to join George Bernard Shaw and Edward Carpenter in the Social Democratic Federation devotes a whole chapter of his reminiscences to what he scornfully calls the Latin Verse Manufactory. Endearingly he allows the reader to perceive that he was himself something of an artist in the medium. Salt, it may be argued, was a visionary who wished to transform society, Eton necessarily included, into something that no one would recognize and few could imagine. But the same can hardly be said of A.C. Benson who expressed himself no less forcibly

'But the classics are poor pabulum, I fear. I live in dread of the public finding out how bad an education is the only one I can communicate. We do nothing to train fancy, memory, taste, imagination; we do not stimulate. We only make the ordinary boy hate and despise books and knowledge generally; but we make them conscientious – good drudges, I think.'[24]

That was written towards the end of an exhausting school year. A little later when he had resigned from Eton in order to edit Queen Victoria's Letters he wrote in retrospect:

'... the *purposelessness* of so much; that was what knocked the bottom out of the Eton life for me. To feel that for nine-tenths of one's furiously busy hours one was teaching boys what they had better not learn, and what could do them no good

24 *The Diary of A.C. Benson* (ed. Lubbock) (1926), 39.

drumming in the letter, & leaving the spirit to take care of itself.'[25]

It could be objected that Benson, by his own confession and in the considered judgment of so old a friend and colleague as Luxmoore, was not himself a scholar, did not live by and for the standards of scholarship. But what about Cory and his phrase already quoted: 'Absurd as the Eton schooling was . . .' How is that to be laughed off?

Of course it can't be. If teachers of the quality of Benson and Cory could not succeed to their own satisfaction, who could? Clearly for many, probably for most, of those who endured the classical training in its full rigour, boredom and futility were the strongest impressions left on the mind. Indeed even those who look back on it with a lifetime's gratitude, as the present writer does, will remember no small share of these sentiments. All this, however, is implicit in the defence of any advanced or ambitious study. Or, to extend the argument to its widest, to the pursuit of excellence in anything. As Luxmoore put it: 'You can't train sound hard-headed men on kindergarten methods.' Even Benson in the passage quoted admits that the system, indefensible as he thinks it, does train its initiates (or would bulldoze them be a more appropriate expression?) into habits of conscientiousness. That other disciplines may achieve these results is not disputed. That the classical system maintained its primacy at Eton more because it was established in fact than because it was recognized to be superior in theory is highly probable. But all this does not dispose of the fact that Cory, with some misgivings, and Luxmoore, with none, believed it to be the best: and that Benson, who didn't, felt his standards to be inferior even though he knew himself able to awaken the interest and stimulate the faculties that, in his view, the classics numbed. Perhaps the truth is that scholarship like unselfishness or courage in battle is transmitted by example, touches people without their knowing it and animates them to act or think in a way that they would not have done from their own resources and cannot without embarrassment reconcile to their everyday professions.

25 *ibid*, 98.

Whatever the explanation the fact of this tradition of scholarship, of the pursuit of knowledge, of intellectual excellence, lies at the heart of Eton in the century that ended with the Second World War. Money and fashion and snobbery, the associations so easily evoked by the mention of the place, meant nothing to the men, a dozen or two at most, whose most eminent exemplars have been discussed in this chapter. The pupils whom they influenced learned to despise such things. The tone they set remained a characteristic note, sometimes rising, sometimes falling, but never drowned. Of course the people who came to the school hankering after these things, caring nothing for sound learning and less for religion, found what they brought with them. But why did they bring it there in the first place? Surely for the same reason that visitors have spread noise and vulgarity and ugliness along the shores of the Mediterranean. Beauty, especially unspoilt beauty, is, it appears, psychologically disturbing to those who deny its value. And Eton in the period here discussed held its own against philistinism better than Provence or the Costa Brava has managed in the last few decades.

Civilization is a struggle of the few against the many. Thermopylae inspired the best epitaph ever written because it gave matchless expression to this ever recurring image. Even within civilized societies the same is true. What gave Eton its power of resistance to the cult of games and colours that swept in an engulfing tide over the late Victorian public school was the tradition of scholarship, the insistence on the cultivation of taste in literature and the arts, and the fastidiousness that flowed from this.

Games resolved so many of the problems inherent in segregating some hundreds of boys for two-thirds of the year that it is not surprising that once established as part of the regular life and discipline of the school they should soon have come to dominate it. Idleness, indiscipline, drunkenness, bullying, fighting, all these and other even less desirable pursuits were vastly reduced by the mere siphoning off of time and energy to the playing fields, the fives courts and the river. The advantages to health were obvious and those to morality were rapidly discerned in that golden age of muscular Christianity. Dr Newsome has shown in his *Godliness and Good Learning* how the moral energy released by Dr Arnold's famous headmastership of Rugby was perverted, with the best of good intentions, into the cult of manliness by his less intellectual admirers, among them the author of *Tom Brown's Schooldays.* At Eton both Hornby and Warre were strongly sympathetic, especially Warre, to the collective, non-individualist character of the team spirit. In the sixties the first masters were appointed whose real function, not openly admitted by the terms of their employment, was to teach games, in particular cricket. But this was still an élitist pursuit. Their pupils were to be the Eleven which since the beginning of the century had challenged Harrow and Westminster to public matches. As Edward Lyttelton himself a notable Captain of the Eleven pointed out in his reminiscences it was not until 1887 that pitches were reluctantly allotted to general use. Stimulated by the growth of organized games at the universities the whole apparatus of house colours, school colours and choices sprang into luxuriant life. From having far too few games it was a bare ten years or so before there were too many, taking up too much time and concentrating too much attention.

Cory, Ainger, Luxmoore and their friends were too steeped in Greek ideas to think of opposing athleticism. Cory wrote the words for the Eton Boating Song and endowed a House Cricket Cup. Ainger built fives courts at his own expense. Luxmoore would be on the touchline cheering on his house football team as any Greek citizen would have done in analogous circumstances. They knew, too, what Eton had been like before games were generally available and they welcomed them. But they were enemies to philistinism, contemptuous of the foppery of colours and disliked the conversion of the Eton Society, in whose debates Gladstone had won his spurs, into a pantheon sacred to both these regrettable tendencies. Gay coloured waistcoats, sponge bag trousers, sealing wax on the brims of top hats, braided edges to tail coats, distinguished a membership now largely composed of successful games-players. It was, of course, enthusiastically approved by the vast majority of boys. Indeed it represented an almost perfect expression of puerility.

As such it also commended itself to those masters who had never wished to grow up.

Benson, it should be said, was suspicious and contemptuous of all athleticism and especially passionate in his denunciation of 'this odious wet-bobbing'. As a conscientious housemaster he recognised the necessity for some success at games but the sight of his colleagues on the touchline is characteristically rendered: 'a lot of listless beaks, incapable of walking, talking or even smiling, looking drearily on in aquascuta, like opium eaters'.

So for a great number of the boys from the last years of the nineteenth century the life of the place centred on the opportunities it offered to those who were good at ball games or showed promise on the river. In so far as this was true Eton conformed to the general type of public school.[26] In so far as it was not most of the credit belongs to the men discussed in this chapter and to those whom they attracted to their tradition. At the age of 85 Luxmoore wrote to an ex-pupil, then a prominent politician, who had questioned the educational creed by which he had lived:

> About the 'Verses' have I any excuse? I still think there is no way of starting a youngster to invent, so good as giving a neat little tuneful trellis & a bald idea to expand up to it. The English Essay is reams of 'piffle', the latin essay far more difficult & far more disliked. The mistake for you was to suppose you needed any stimulus or help for invention. It only cramped you, already an author ... Our fault is that the Classics are so badly taught (were so by me) & smothered in Grammar (wh. after all is science).[27]

Late nineteenth-century Eton was diversified and extended by its contrasts. It had become a great games-playing school whose cricketers could take their place in a first-class side and whose oarsmen carried off trophies at Henley. But it was also a school with a strong flavour of the university: its boys, except

26 So entertainingly illuminated in the writings of Dr Newsome and Mr Honey and so painstakingly (and disapprovingly) anatomised in the works of Edward G. Mack.
27 *Letters*, 344.

for the most junior Collegers who still spent their first year in a modified, sanitised Long Chamber, all had rooms of their own. In Oppidan houses each had its own fireplace, emblem of privacy and domesticity. The tutorial system cultivated individuality: aestheticism and intellectual curiosity could find a lodging there and had, as we have seen, powerful champions. In religion external observances were maintained at the old level. Chapel was compulsory except for Jews and Roman Catholics. Besides a brief morning service each weekday attendance was required at both mattins and evensong on Sundays, the former usually extended by a sermon. Boredom justified what H.S. Salt called 'the pleasant heathenism of Eton'. But here again there was a strong tradition of personal piety among those masters who read and thought. Men such as Cory and Benson who found themselves unable to make a Christian profession of faith certainly did not regard themselves as irreligious or encourage their pupils towards unbelief. They were exasperated by parsonical fatuities but they were far from embracing the cheerful materialism that their colleague Salt so much approved.

Again in the content of the education offered there were tensions. The classics were still in a position of overwhelming superiority but their most distinguished exponents were precisely those who favoured expansion and reform. Cory had given evidence to the Royal Commission in favour of broadening the curriculum and improving the status of masters teaching mathematics and French. Luxmoore had encouraged the study of the fine arts and over many years made the membership of the society devoted to the reading of Shakespeare, founded by his friend Warre Cornish, one of the most enriching of Eton experiences.

The most valuable feature of this plurality was that it engendered a spirit, if not of opposition, at least of rational and independent criticism. It was not non-conformity so much as non-acceptance. Particularly strong in College but fostered by the tutors in the Cory tradition, themselves old Collegers, it was a powerful solvent of the sentimental complacency to which venerable and successful institutions are prone. There is even a redeeming example of this in an otherwise embarrassingly mawkish book, Hugh Macnaghten's *Fifty Years of Eton*. Macnaghten was in College when Warre was still a housemaster and shared with his fellow scholars an irreverent impatience towards Warre's preoccupation with the Corps. One day the Corps was drilling within earshot of College and one of the scholars took advantage of this to confuse its evolutions by shouting mischievous commands through a window. Warre was extremely angry and 'told some boy that this could only have happened in College, and the boy repeated it to me. Consequently when I was sent for as Captain of the School to extradite the guilty I went in the wrong spirit and made things worse. It was largely due to the kind offices of the master in College that Warre after some days forgave me.'[28] Warre clinched his moral victory by inviting Macnaghten to dinner a few weeks later to meet General Roberts, fresh from his brilliant relief of Kandahar. Few boys could have resisted so flattering a conversion, reinforced as it was by the charm and generosity of Warre's nature. Macnaghten survived to become an apologist for all things Etonian in terms so extravagant as to evoke distaste, or even hostility. But the spirit by which he was touched in his boyhood was to make itself felt more strongly in the years that followed.

28 *op. cit.* 58. The offender whose identity Macnaghten was at such pains to conceal was, it appears, none other than the future Provost, M.R. James. See *Eton and King's,* 70 – 1, where a circumstantial account suggests that it was not shouting contrary commands but drowning those given by beating a hip bath with a rubber siphon that was the means employed.

CHAPTER SIX

———————∽———————

The Impact
of the First World War

IN WARRE'S SUCCESSOR AS HEAD MASTER, Edward Lyttelton, the Governing Body chose a product of these conflicting tendencies. A famous Captain of the Eleven and one of the most elegant batsmen of his day, he was far from holding the safe and tried opinions of his predecessor. A nephew of Gladstone whose first administration had coincided with his own schooltime he had been a pupil of H.S. Salt. Salt transcribes with glee an empurpled passage that appeared in the *Eton College Chronicle* when, in 1908, the Head Master invited an unemployed workman to address the school from the chapel steps. The twentieth century had entered School Yard.

Lyttelton's headmastership was important for what it represented rather than for what it was. Perhaps the same might be said of the man himself. He epitomised so much that was specifically Etonian: he belonged to a family whose association with the school was more continuously distinguished than any other; his father had been one of the earliest Newcastle examiners in the same year as Gladstone; his younger brother Alfred, perhaps the most widely admired and loved figure of his generation, was the best all-round athlete the school had ever produced and one of the greatest cricketers in the history of the game (to have one's play described by W.G. Grace as 'the champagne of cricket' is surely a distinction besides which entry to the Cabinet after less than ten years on the back benches fades into the light of common day); his half-sister was the wife of Cyril Alington who was to succeed him as Head Master; his nephew George was to be among the best known and longest serving Eton master of the first half of the twentieth century. He was a devout Christian, at least in intention and in external observance, if not in the strictest sense of credal orthodoxy. His old pupil Geoffrey Madan has left a charming picture of him on a bicycling tour with a couple of Eton boys and his friend the vicar of Pershore:

'As darkness came on he would read evensong, accompanied by the vicar of Pershore, on his knees in the Commercial Room of the village inn. Rustic figures would gape and stare, pipe or glass in hand, while through the mist of smoke and fumes of drink his deep booming voice would answer the confident crackle of the Vicar.'[1]

'The Brown Man' as he was affectionately known to his family in allusion to his deep tan was an eccentric. He was thus inevitably suspect in the eyes of the *bien pensants* and, at least potentially, an ally of independents and radicals. But he was not, unlike almost all his predecessors, a man of learning. 'Edward' wrote Geoffrey Madan in the memoir already quoted 'was no scholar; indeed his mind turned like a needle to the pole, to whatever was the reverse of scholarship. Yet it would never relax the will to grasp and to expound. Whether in classics or theology, his teaching was positively corrosive of sound learning and only less so of religion; but there was no failure of effort on his own part. He inspired great mistrust in what he taught, but greater devotion to himself.'

This want of coherence, of intellectual force, aborted his initiatives and prevented his liberality of spirit from making the impact that it should have done. He is remembered (if he is remembered at all) as a failure because he was forced to resign after the outcry he occasioned by a sermon preached in 1916, urging the possibility of a negotiated peace and suggesting the surrender of Gibraltar as an earnest of the country's intention to lead a new political life according to the commandments of God. The expedient proposed was idiotic but the essential idea was not ignoble. A year later it was put forward in a more rational and statesmanlike manner by Lord Lansdowne in the

1 *Etoniana* 121/330.

famous letter which both *The Times* and the *Morning Post* refused to print. It appeared therefore in the *Daily Telegraph* on Friday November 29th 1917. On the very next day the Old Etonian Association was to hold its annual meeting at Eton to elect its President for the coming year. Contested elections were by custom avoided: only one candidate had been nominated and that was Lord Lansdowne, an ex-Fellow of Eton as well as a past Governor-General of Canada, Viceroy of India and Foreign Secretary. In spite of these distinctions, in spite of the moderate tone of Lord Lansdowne's proposals, the outrage of suggesting an accommodation with Germany was too much. But what was to be done? There was no time to reconvene the Committee and put forward another name. The Chairman, acting on his own responsibility, refused to move Lord Lansdowne's nomination and proposed another mute inglorious Marquess who was instantly elected.[2]

It is perhaps permissible to distinguish between this storm in Old Etonian teacups and the termination of Edward Lyttelton's headmastership. War or no war it is hard to believe that this would have run its full term. It was not so much that his ideas were preposterous (though some of them were) as that he was. Yet much that he did, and more that he stood for, was admirable. For flogging he substituted beating, a much milder and less humiliating form of corporal punishment. The first was inflicted with the birch on the bare bottom; the second with the cane on the clothed (and perhaps padded) posterior. He carried the tradition of Cory and of Luxmoore into the seat of authority, never standing on the dignity of his position or making boys feel that they were in the presence of royalty, if not of a still higher order of being. His obvious contempt for snobbery and his readiness to question the established order of society were as valuable as they were timely. Such attitudes were, as we have seen, an important part of the Eton tradition but the support of the Head Master was a notable reinforcement. Or should have been. At the very least the boys had been given the opportunity of listening to an unemployed workman in School Yard and

2 *ibid* 113/198.

among an audience of that age there would have been at least some generosity, some sympathetic imagination, so noticeably lacking in the infuriated Old Etonians who wrote to the *Chronicle*.

Had Lyttelton not been chosen, Warre's successor would almost certainly have been his own preferred candidate, A.C. Benson. But was Benson a candidate? The Governing Body had difficulty in making out. Had he declared himself all the evidence suggests that he would have been elected. At the interview the Provost, Hornby, was compelled to ask him bluntly whether he would accept the post if offered. Benson's answer 'In that case I feel the offer should *not* be made' could only be taken as a refusal. Yet it seems clear that that was not the end of the matter. He was sent details of the salary and perquisites, £4,750 a year together with a house and other allowances, and one of the Fellow wrote privately to ask him his real intentions. Only then did he make a categorical refusal;[3] and even then he seems to have felt some resentment against Eton for not having dragged him, like St Ambrose, protesting to his enthronement. Although he had old and close friends there he shook its dust from his feet and did not revisit it for ten years.

Probably his real grievance was that his ex-colleagues had failed to elect him to the Governing Body as Masters' Representative when he offered himself as a candidate soon after Lyttelton's appointment. In his heart he knew himself to be temperamentally unfitted for the headmastership. The evidence of his diary in many entries over a long period consistently attests this. So does his actual behaviour when asked if he wished to stand. But a Fellowship was quite another matter. He would have welcomed the distinction it conferred and may well have thought that he had a better right to it than most. Not only had he been a highly successful and popular master, he had championed the down-trodden non-classical beaks in the great controversy at the beginning of the century over their right to succeed to a house. No doubt it was this, aggravated by his

3 Newsome. *On the edge of Paradise*, 180.

outspoken scepticism as to the virtues of a classical education, that turned the votes of his old friends against him.[4]

When he did come back, in 1916, it was to say goodbye to his old colleague Warre Cornish, the Vice-Provost, who was dying. His reflections, set down with the sharp freshness of a born diarist, open another view of the school and of his relation to it:

'Drove down in soft sunshine along the old streets; the first sight of the boys in the ridiculous dress – yet looking so hand-some and fine, many of them – moved me a good deal.

'I certainly could not have had a sweeter day to revisit the old affair: twenty-seven years of my life – i.e. exactly half so far – spent there. I had some happiness there as a boy, but no experience, and as a master some experience and not much happiness. But it isn't my native air at all. It represents an aristocratic life, a life pursuing *knightly* virtues – chivalry, agility, honour, something Spartan. I am not like that at all; I like the poetical, epicurean, tranquil, semi-monastic life. I haven't the clean, fresh sinfulness of the Knight; I am half bourgeois, half monk. I was never big enough to embrace and overlap Eton. This could be done by a large-hearted and fatherly man, because it has the petulant and inconsiderate faults of youth; and such an one could have extended to it a fatherly and amused tolerance. But I was always a little afraid of it and its mockery, without ever respecting its ideals. I was glad to get away. Now that I go back after a gap, I see its pretty paces and ornaments – it bounds along like a greyhound – it has no virtues, only some instincts.'[5]

The visit was poignant, not only from the reviving of old memories or from the undimmed courtesy and wit of his stricken friend: 'Presently men came and took Cornish out of his armchair and put him in a carrying chair – He said to me with a smile, "It is so strange to be carried about in a tray." ' The Vice-Provost was transferred to a bathchair. Accompanied by his wife and Benson they went out of the cloisters into the playing fields. This gave an opening for a *coup-de-théâtre*: 'In the

4 I owe this suggestion to Walter Hamilton.
5 *Diary* ed. Lubbock, 286.

playing fields we saw, in Poet's Walk, a white-haired woodman, wielding an axe over the postrate trees. "Who is that fine-looking old man?" said Mrs Cornish. A group of boys were watching him curiously and derisively. It was Edward Lyttelton!. . .' Benson knew that the letter of resignation, following the notorious sermon, had been sent and accepted. He had not been to Eton between the moment when he was himself vacillating over his own candidacy and the time when the head-mastership was once again vacant. So accomplished a literary artist could hardly pass by such tempting material. Eton was once again available. Is it fanciful to see in so vigorous a rejection of her charms an exorcism of a haunting desire as well as a rationalisation of a past decision? Certainly Benson firmly resisted any suggestion that he might offer himself and at once supported the general view that Cyril Alington, Headmaster of Shrewsbury and previously Master in College at Eton, was the obvious choice.

The choice in 1905 had lain between two men neither of whom was accounted a scholar or a safe man. Benson had never concealed his scepticism as to the value of the Eton classical training or his intention of changing it if he were put in charge. Lyttelton thought the real importance of education to be moral and social, not intellectual. He did not, in fact, undermine the commanding position of the classics but he easily might have done if the whim had taken him. Some of the initiatives he did take were both valuable and courageous. Even under Hornby the Governing Body had shown themselves well disposed towards potential innovators. In the following decade the great Liberal victory of 1905, the social and financial policies champ-ioned by Lloyd George and Winston Churchill had perhaps not gone unnoticed by the Fellows of Eton who were, under the remodelled statues, men of affairs not remote clerical pensioners.

When Lyttelton resigned the Provost was no longer Hornby but Warre, a Warre sadly reduced by age and ill-health from the majestic figure who had towered benignly over the school in the days of his headmastership. The effective head of the Govern-ing Body was the Senior Fellow, M.R. James, who had been

94

Provost of King's since 1905 and was to succeed Warre as Provost of Eton in 1918. The combination of Cyril Alington as Head Master and James as Provost was thus all but synchronous. Alington was appointed Head Master in January 1917 and left to become Dean of Durham in 1933. James was installed as Provost on Michaelmas Day 1918 and died in office in June 1936. Their relations were as happy as any in the history of Eton, so that their very different qualities were mutually enhanced. No doubt this harmony owed much to a personality as strongly marked as either and in power of attraction perhaps superior, that of Hester Alington, the Head Master's wife. Certainly no previous occupant of her position had had any comparable influence on masters and boys, indeed on the place itself since her extraordinary humanity observed no limits or categories. The College workmen who kept the cloisters in repair, the railway porters who retrieved her errant possessions enjoyed her generosity of spirit, amused and amusing, as much as the nervous newcomers to staff and school who found themselves at once, and miraculously, at home. Three of the boys who went through the school in her time became her sons-in-law, one of whom, Lord Home, has sketched her character and her wit with felicitous economy.[6] Henry Green, another contemporary, singles out her goodness and kindness in an autobiography that otherwise paints Eton as a worthless, unhappy place.[7] When she came to the school only four of the masters were married.[8] The acceptance of women in so overwhelmingly masculine a society was made easy by her civilizing presence.

The old celibate tradition of the ancient universities and their annexed foundations was personified at its most uncomplicated and at its most winning in the new Provost, M.R. James. Like Mrs Alington, he was unencumbered by any sense of his own importance. Sir Robert Birley, then a young master, recalls finding the Provost sitting on the ground in the playing fields

6 Home, *The Way the Wind Blows*, 55 – 6.
7 *Pack my Bag* (1940 n.e. 1979), 148 – 9.
8 Information from Mrs Hartley, who came to Eton in 1922 as the wife of a master.

with an inexplicably purposeful air. It transpired that a small
boy looking for a lost ball had suddenly remembered that he
was due to answer his name at absence and had charged the
mild-looking passer-by to mark the spot.[9] It was the special
grace of the Provost's nature that he should invite such a trust,
that he should instantly accept it and that he should always give
the impression of having all the time in the world for anyone
who cared to approach him. Even the great Lord Acton had
been mystified by this.

'Is it true,' he had asked one of James's brother Fellows at
King's, 'that he is ready to spend every evening playing games
or talking with undergraduates?'

'Yes, the evenings and more.'

'And do you know that in knowledge of MSS he is already
third or fourth in Europe?'

'I am interested to hear you say so, sir.'

'Then how does he manage it?'

'We have not yet found out.'[10]

He took the secret with him. Even his sympathetic and scholarly biographer does not altogether explain it though he gives the
best exposition we are ever likely to have of the range and
quality of the Provost's scholarship. This lay in the vast but
then little explored fields of the apocryphal gospels, early Christian writings which had not won admission to the New Testament although they purported to be of the same nature and
origins as those that were, and of medieval iconography. The
Provost's knowledge of this last subject was by no means
limited to illuminated manuscripts, where his reputation had so
impressed Lord Acton, but comprehended the whole range of
stained glass, wall paintings, sculpture and wood carving to be
found in the great churches, and many of the not so great
churches, of Western Europe. In the large territory where these
two studies overlapped he was without a rival. Time and again
he was able to demonstrate the significance of the scenes depic-
ted in a fresco or a misericord by reference to the stories with

9 Personal communication to the author.
10 quot. Pfaff, *Montague Rhodes James*, 128.

which the medieval mind teemed but which had their origins in the apocryphal gospels or other uncanonical writings.

The qualities of mind required by the study of material so diffuse, so disparate, so remote from the well-lit streets of scholarship are rare. There must first of all be largeness, comprehensiveness, not only of understanding but of appetite. 'I believe there never was a time when I had more of a programme than to find out all I could about various matters and to make friends' he had written in what his biographer tells us was 'one of the few genuinely introspective personal letters he ever wrote as an adult.'[11] It is love of learning, curiosity about a subject for its own sake rather than an ambition to make a name as a scholar or to establish some new orthodoxy, that remains his motive from first to last. And then there is sympathy with and respect for people who were simple and uneducated. Knowingness and superciliousness disable a man from the kind of understanding that M.R. James was seeking. Enjoyment of a story, as a child enjoys a story, is another qualification that not every scholar can command. It was not for nothing that the Provost had early established himself, where he has ever since remained, as one of the most accomplished practitioners of the ghost story.

All of these are qualities of mind, even perhaps of character, distinct from the technical abilities and acquired skills that make up a scholar. They are thus relevant to any consideration of M.R. James in his capacity as Provost and of his influence on the place. His biographer in the estimate of his scholarship already referred to draws attention to two elements in it that are also pertinent in this connexion. One he happily describes as 'the strengths of his Latinity' which he defines as 'a thorough knowledge of the possibilities of the Latin language at any given point and a sense of how his author's mind might have been working'. The second half of this definition is an expansion of what Professor Pfaff calls 'his flair for the unusual and the distinctive'. But the dependence of the second quality on the first is clear. One cannot tell what is unusual unless one is very thoroughly at home with the potentialites of the medium, in this

11 *ibid*, vii.

case the Latin language. And this he owed, in Professor Pfaff's words, to 'the soundness of his classical training at Eton'.[12]

The second strength was that he knew his Bible not only with the accuracy and critical sense of a born scholar but with the perceptions and recognitions of a man who had steadily and earnestly tried to live by it. In both these respects the Provost brought back to Eton, with added lustre, what he had taken with him when he left. It was therefore safe to conclude that any proposal to forsake the classics for the pursuit of more modern studies or to disestablish the chapel and the teaching of Christianity in favour of instruction in ethics or comparative religion would not attract his support. Yet there appears to have been no trace of religiosity or rigidity about him. His father, to whom as to all his family, he was very close in affection had pressed him with all the zeal of a lifelong Evangelical to follow his example in taking Holy Orders. Several of his intimate friends, among them his old tutor, Luxmoore, urged him to consider it. Doubtless he did so. It is impossible to imagine so dutiful and unselfseeking a man taking such a decision lightly. But he seems never to have felt any such vocation.

The depth and certainty of his convictions did not issue in a desire to impose them on others. 'Your influence would be conservative without bigotry' wrote his brother, encouraging him to let his name be put forward for the Provostship of King's in 1905.[13] The true temper of his mind is evident from a remark in his introduction to one of the most remarkable of his manuscript discoveries: 'The phenomenon of the preservation of the most heretical portion of a heretical and condemned book in a fourteenth century MS is a very noteworthy and encouraging one, as well as one which is difficult to explain.'[14] He was a conservative not from narrow views or selfish motives but because he loved and valued what had been entrusted to him to conserve. Tranquil by temperament (he seems never to have been in love and, on the evidence of his editorial practice, to

12 *ibid*, 230.
13 *ibid* 210.
14 *ibid* quot. f[n] 105, p. 157.

have regarded sex in all its forms as a bodily function that no properly brought up person should mention) and tolerant by principle, he reflected the happy, useful, serious virtues of the late Victorian age. He had gone to Eton as a scholar in 1876 and to King's in 1882. For the next thirty years he had enjoyed an England and a Europe that to the general view offered an unbroken prospect of peace and prosperity. The capricious anarchy of the middle ages, the wars of religion of the sixteenth and seventeenth centuries, the less destructive but still almost continuous warfare of the eighteenth century issuing at last in the great struggle that had begun with the French Revolution and ended with the defeat of Napolean – these things had gone for good. Or so it seemed. A young scholar corresponding with learned men all over Europe met only courtesy and civility. Since these qualities were instinctive to M.R. James it was natural to assume them as part of the modern world, like proper sanitation or a regular police force.

The shock of the 1914 – 18 war was the more profound. Its griefs and horrors were on a scale that neither imagination could compass nor experience console. And it struck on the consciousness, the moral consciousness particularly, of the older generation because it seemed to them that one nation, Germany, had wilfully turned back to what the world had at long last escaped from. So clear an attribution of historical guilt would now find few defenders. But it was widely accepted at the time that M.R. James became Provost of Eton, and he, like many of his fellow scholars, certainly and unequivocally accepted it.[15]

Eton and King's had suffered bitter losses. The slaughter of so many young men, mere boys often, was heart-rending for the housemaster and College tutors. If, as they believed, responsibility for this could be established beyond reasonable doubt, they would have been less, or perhaps more, than human if anger and resentment had not fed on their grief. These emotions, smouldering beneath the exhausted incredulity of the Armistice, would sometimes blaze out. C.R.L. Fletcher, one of

15 *ibid* 335 – 6

the men who shaped the Oxford History School, had left College in the year that M.R. James had arrived there. During the war, in which he had lost two of his three sons, he had returned to teach history at the school (he had volunteered for the RNVR at the age of fifty-seven, had been accepted but had been discharged with lumbago caused by scrubbing floors at a London depot). Was it surprising that such a man should refuse to attend any old Colleger function if he thought that he might have to meet, and be civil to, Maynard Keynes? Keynes had combined a somewhat equivocal attitude to the war[16] with advising the government on the financing of it. His *Economic Consequences of the Peace* was the first, and most brilliant, attempt to cast a defeated Germany in the role of babe in the wood with Lloyd George and Clemenceau as the wicked uncles. The days when he would write to the *New Statesman* to thank heaven for Colonel Blimp were not yet.

Even without the war and its envenoming of antipathies there were signs that the old consensus was in danger. In King's two fissiparous forces had coalesced: those released by the crisis of religious belief and those generated by the reform of the College, most notably by opening its entry to non-Etonians. In any institution there will always be a dividing line between the long established and the newly arrived. In a college whose members form one household, dining at the same table and sharing the same rooms for reading the newspapers and gossiping with each other, there will be a sharpened awareness of standing, of belonging. If this is further underlined by a radical alteration of the whole basis of membership, a basis that had hitherto guaranteed a huge common area of experience and convention, a division will be created that only tact, goodwill and good manners can bridge. Academic persons are not as a rule conspicuous for these qualities. Indeed their analytic and critical training predisposes them to be touchy. The Fellows of King's seem not to have escaped their calling's snare. The Old

16 Clive Bell *Old Friends*, 46, asserts that Keynes was, like himself, a conscientious objector. His biographer, Roy Harrod, makes it plain that this was not the case but gives a somewhat perplexing account of Keynes's behaviour when summoned to register for military service.

Etonians were, or were taken to be, patronizing and exclusive: the newcomers felt themselves to be slighted. A rift in its origins social and accidental became, as these things do, a polarisation of more general significance. It offered, ready made, a party system for serious issues; and in nineteenth century Cambridge religious conformity was the most serious of all. Great figures such as Henry Sidgwick and Leslie Stephen had resigned their fellowships because they could not conscientiously make the professions of belief required of them.

To this tradition Keynes was the natural heir. He had been born and bred in Cambridge where his father was one of the first dons to teach economics and later held the chief administrative office of the university. By the time he came back as an undergraduate with an Eton scholarship in both classics and mathematics the great battles were over. But to Keynes and his circle, the young men of advanced opinions who were to form the nucleus of Bloomsbury, religious belief was a hateful thing, ridiculous in itself and poisonous in its effects. It was not only an intellectual duty but an active pleasure to destroy it and to discomfit its adherents.

Essentially James and Keynes, Eton and King's men of the truest, lightest blue, were the champions of two irreconcilable traditions. James would never pick a quarrel with anyone and if he found himself challenged would make courtesy to his adversary his first concern. Keynes delighted in intellectual combat and was, in his biographer's admiring phrase 'a great past-master in the art of rudeness'. James had, characteristically, made it his aim during his time as Tutor and Dean to heal the divisions of the College. No doubt this explains why his colleagues chose him as their Provost. In that capacity he admitted Keynes to a fellowship within a year of his own election. For a time all went smoothly. James had been hospitable and encouraging to Keynes, as to so many others, in his undergraduate days. But it soon became obvious that Keynes was building up a party that meant to make the College a very different place. The first battles were fought on matters of management and money where Keynes's victory in argument could hardly be in doubt whichever way a vote might go. This was in 1912, six years after Keynes's election. The war brought College life to a standstill. The vacancy at Eton in 1918 offered an honourable escape from the acrimony that to James was the negation of the collegiate idea.

No other Provost of King's in nearly five hundred years had migrated to Eton, in marked contrast to the sister foundation of William of Wykeham where from the late-seventeenth to the mid-eighteenth century the Wardens of New College regularly moved on to Winchester. Once it was known that James would accept the post all rivals faded into the background. The two most influential Old Etonians in the Cabinet, Curzon and A.J. Balfour, would have preferred either Rosebery or Balfour's younger brother Gerald: but neither was thought likely to accept. Rosebery himself told Stamfordham, the King's private secretary, that he favoured A.J. Balfour, who was not in fact available, but did not think Gerald the right man. Both Rosebery and Stamfordham thought James dull but agreed with A.J. Balfour that he was an obviously eligible candidate.[17] Professor Pfaff, James's biographer, suggests a name not mentioned in the correspondence between the ministers and the private secretary, that of W.R. Inge, then and for many years Dean of St Paul's. Inge had belonged to the same election as A.C. Benson and had won distinction as a classical scholar, as a philosopher and as a theologian. In addition to having held a Fellowship at Oxford and a Professorship at Cambridge he had been for four years a master at Eton. Renowned for his incisive, epigrammatic style and for his caustic wit he was hardly the man to over-praise his colleagues. His testimony to the quality of Eton in the late nineteenth century is thus the more telling;

> Of the assistant Masters I can only record my opinion that though since I have lived in London I have seen something of most of our leading men in Church and State, I have never

---

17 Correspondence in the Curzon papers now housed in the India Office Library, MSS Eur. F. 112/121 f.13. I am grateful to Mr Kenneth Rose for making his transcripts available to me, and to Lord Scarsdale for his permission.

met more able and competent men than Edward Leigh, Luxmoore, Ainger, Cornish and Rawlins.[18]

It is impossible to think of an Etonian eminent for scholarship,
however loyal to his old school, making such a judgment, or
anything remotely approaching it, at the beginning of that
century.

Thus the Eton to which Alington came as Head Master and
M.R. James as Provost was a place with a tradition of intellectual quality and of a love of learning that any university might
be proud of. Its beauty and its antiquity, the royal and
aristocratic connexions that made it a magnet for snobbery and
gossip need no further rehearsal but in any estimate of the place
at any time, the best or the worst, there is no forgetting them.
Like climate and situation they are constants, both supporting
and setting limits to the possibilities of life. What was special to
the period between the wars was that it saw the full flowering
of seeds broadcast by William Johnson Cory and those whom
he had inspired. Luxmoore who had felt his influence so deeply
as a young master was still living in Eton: and M.R. James was
Luxmoore's most devoted pupil.

The other characteristic of the period that distinguishes it
from any other is simply this: that it followed the unimaginable
shock of the First World War. The effect of this on men of the
Provost's generation has been suggested. But it reached across
every age of Etonian down to the boys who had been resigned
to accepting slaughter as their natural expectation of life. Before
a horror so universal, so immediate and so huge, imagination
and analysis retire scorched. But it is impossible to read or to
think about Eton in those years during and after the war,
without hearing silences or feeling absences somehow more
insistent than anything that is said or that meets the eye.

18 *Eton Review*, July 1933. I owe this reference to Mr Kenneth Rose.

CHAPTER SEVEN

M. R. James and the Alingtons

CYRIL ALINGTON, THE HEAD MASTER during all but the last three years of James's Provostship, was one of the best equipped of all holders of that office. He was clever, amusing, a witty and a graceful speaker and a writer whose clear and easy prose must yet give place to the merits of his verse, inventive, musical, sure in touch, as pleasing to the fancy as to the ear. He was good at games and enjoyed them to the full without exaggerating their place in the scheme of things. He was a strikingly handsome man with an actor's sense of audience and occasion. He had crowned a run of scholarships with a First in Greats and a Fellowship at All Souls. He was, by the evidence of pupils and colleagues, a teacher of real brilliance: vivid, stimulating, fertile, unexpected. As a preacher he put all these talents at the service of a faith whose obvious sincerity disconcerted those who thought him glib and facile. His evening addresses in College Chapel during Holy Week might be classed among the most effective uses of the pulpit during the twentieth century.

He was too quicksilver a personality to command the universal loyalty and affection that his wife or the Provost did. A man of strong likes and dislikes is apt to find these reciprocated. Yet as a young master in College – the housemaster in charge of the seventy scholars – he won the friendship of some most acute and fastidious judges, Ronald Knox and Patrick Shaw Stewart among them. He had been a master at Eton for nine years, leaving in 1908 to become Headmaster of Shrewsbury.

What is most striking about him is his apparently limitless nervous energy. Besides discharging with evident enthusiasm his duties as Head Master, as a teacher and as a preacher whose services were much in demand outside his own school, he was also an author of enviable productivity. Detective stories, light novels, works of popular theology, even of political history poured from his pen. Articles in the *Evening Standard* and letters to *The Times* appeared in bewildering profusion. Retirements, seventieth birthdays, departures on promotion of members of his staff were celebrated in the *Eton College Chronicle* in verse that lilts and skips beside the ponderosities of schoolboy leading articles and of adult reports of house football matches. Even this incessant and miscellaneous literary output still left him, apparently, fresh and eager for the ordinary pleasures of life. He liked playing and watching games. He enjoyed his rubber of bridge after dinner. He travelled with zest. And his entertainment of both boys and masters, much as it owed to the wit and to the welcoming sympathy of his wife, was in itself enough to have justified his headmastership.

His critics found his undoubted fondness for publicity unbecoming. It was easy too to accuse a man who wrote and spoke so often and on so many subjects of shallowness and superficiality, even perhaps of vanity. From there it is a short and tempting passage to the imputation of hypocrisy. Alington was a clever and ambitious man who saw that Eton occupied an unrivalled position in the social and political system of his time. Of course the whole thing was a gigantic sham: useless, out-moded, obstructive of real social and intellectual progress. He was quite clever enough to see that too. But he preferred, like the generality of clever and ambitious people in any age, to play the role of hanger on. Such, more or less obliquely suggested, is the judgment of him to be found in the writings of Connolly and Orwell who were in College during the first years of his headmastership. In both cases the authors were writing some fifteen or more years after they had any contact with him and from a professedly left-wing position that neither had held as a schoolboy and that Connolly soon abandoned. Neither would have included M.R. James or Luxmoore in the same condemnation. They belonged to the past. Alington was a rational and astute denizen of the modern world.

Some of the more old-fashioned Eton figures would have agreed with them there. It was very wonderful to have a Head Master who wrote for the evening papers and turned out crime stories but was it quite what was wanted? Like the monarchy and the aristocracy with which it was so intimately associated Eton scented danger in too frequent an intercourse with the Press. Cyril Alington was never out of the papers for long. And the energy of his consciousness pressing on his instinctive articulacy no doubt led him, not so much into indiscretion for which he was too quick-witted and present-minded, but into multiplying opinions beyond what was strictly necessary.

For the ambassadorial, civil servant side of his office this may have been a disadvantage. From the schoolmasterly side it was a breath of fresh air. Safe inaudibility was the last thing he wanted or, perhaps, was capable of. In his teaching as at his dinner parties he enjoyed saying outrageous things to see what reactions he might elicit. He had a sense of humour.

In his preference for clear and challenging opinions, in his enjoyment of innocent mischief, above all in his encouragement of clever boys and his readiness to bear with their occasional tiresomeness Alington was the antithesis of his great predecessor Dr Warre. His agility, his modernity, perfectly complemented the stillness and depth that M.R. James so un-selfconsciously expressed. His shrewdness and knowledge of the world equipped him to train young masters in the tactical necessities of their profession. Sir Robert Birley recalls his skil-ful and instructive handling of a difficulty he himself faced soon after joining the staff at Eton. An older master of notably tyrannical habits bore a grudge against a boy who was coming to Birley for tuition. Wanting an excuse for penalising him he claimed that the work he had been doing was altogether unsatis-factory and singled out this aspect of it to justify severe punish-ment. Birley stood up for his pupil. The older man grew more peremptory and offensive. There was nothing for it but to go to the Head Master. Alington told Birley to conduct his side of the correspondence under his eye (but to come to the Head Master's house equipped with his own writing paper so that the old fox should not get wind of this unusual form of extramural

coaching). The result was the extortion of an apology from a
man who had long ceased to think that the word could have any
reference to his own behaviour.[1]

A.C. Benson had been a firm supporter of Alington's appointment. His sketch of him, taken from his diary at the time,
outlines with his characteristic deftness what later critics and
admirers were to find:

> Alington has a touch of genius and is full of courage: he is
> not, as they say, quite a gentleman, and he has some of
> Creighton's cynicism. But he has much character and fear-
> lessness, and is ambitious enough to run a show well. A.
> poses as unconventional, but I think he is very conventional
> in his ambitions, and just understands the value of stimulat-
> ing curiosity. I should fear him as an adversary rather than
> respect him as an opponent.[2]

Some explanation may be offered of the less flattering details of
this pithy characterisation. Benson was not a snob. Or does he
sometimes protest too much at the dullness and insipidity of the
pleasures and palaces among which he roams? At any rate he
was not a snob in the sense that Sir Walter Elliot of Kellynch
Hall was, and 'not quite a gentleman' is to be understood in
terms of taste, manners and conduct, not of lineage. The cyni-
cism which he qualifies with the name of Mandell Creighton,
the historian and Bishop of London, is an apt identification. Wit
in a parson is often taken as a mark of insincerity. 'No people
do so much harm as those who go about doing good' the single
epigram by which the Bishop is represented in the *Oxford Dic-
tionary of Quotations* lends itself to such an aggrieved interpretation. It is exactly the kind of thing that Alington might have
said if he had thought of it. Perhaps it was not the least valuable
of qualities in a society where philistinism, piety and sentimentality were strongly entrenched.

The philistinism that sprang from the cult of games with its
hierarchy of colours was nourished by the social and economic

---

1 Personal communication from Sir Robert Birley.
2 quot. Newsome *On the Edge of Paradise*, 338.

snobbery of society in general. Money and titles, not intellectual or artistic distinction, still less beauty of character or refinement of spirit, were the objects of general ambition and approval. This had been true of Edwardian England and remained true in the shriller period that followed the war. There was of course nothing specifically Etonian about this phenomenon. But Eton, like all human institutions, must take a great deal of its character from its surroundings. Edward Lyttelton, Alington's predecessor, put the point even more strongly in his autobiography: 'For ... a school always is what society is: far from perfect; amiss just as society is, but in good points more hopeful, as good is seen in process of growth ... Our Public Schools are not the cause of the national character but the symptom of it ... huge groups of the population who know nothing of those schools betray the same qualities, good and bad.'[3] The rich and the well-connected like the poor would in general have much preferred that a son should get into the Eleven than that he should carry off an armful of prizes. The boys themselves, with a tiny number of exceptions, emphatic-ally concurred. The external distinctions of Eton society, what one might wear, where one might go, largely depended on success at games and the privileges that flowed from it. All this is the commonplace of public school literature, not least of its novels and short stories. What is commonplace does not call for extended comment but its weight and influence must be reckoned with. The power of an institution or an individual to transform the values of the herd is in the short run slight.

If philistinism is a constant, and a powerful one, in the world of the public school (as in the world at large) so is, or was, sentimentality. The combination of the two produces the Old School spirit at its most stupefying: stupefying, that is, to the natives but to the foreigner merely nauseous. 'The never to be forgotten final of 1894.' How the rush of excited phrases freezes the circulation. Eton has contributed its fair share to these slag heaps from the furnaces of past loyalty and affection.

If piety is the root of education, a top dressing of scepticism

---

3 *Memories and Hopes*, 19, 46.

helps to keep the plant in health. Alington's readiness to question, to act as a Socratic gadfly and to encourage his pupils to do so, was of all the more value. And if Benson's judgment was right, that at heart he was both conservative and conventional, that was an additional qualification. A man who will only be liberal on the side of his own favourite opinions will hardly encourage the young to spread their wings. On the other hand too diffuse a radicalism stultifies itself. The life of a Head Master of Eton would scarcely be tolerable if every absurdity of custom and usage were to be stopped and challenged at the barrier of reason. It is a great thing to be able to enter into different enjoyments. Both the Provost and the Head Master were conspicuous examples of this happy disposition. Both were intellectuals, if of very different kinds, but both took evident pleasure in the company of all sorts and conditions of boys and in amusements that everyone shared. There was nothing precious or condescending in this. M.R. James's knowledge of light fiction could sometimes startle those who stood in awe of his erudition. His admiration for P.G. Wodehouse was intense. A common friend arranged a visit to the Lodge where the Provost received his guest with such enthusiasm that an invitation to stay to lunch was thought inevitable. As one o'clock drew nearer it was not, however, forthcoming. The great man was conducted to his friend's house and was not a little put out to hear the Provost's lapse from his usual standard of hospitality tersely explained: 'It's Mrs Woodhouse.' It was further explained that this was the name of the Provost's widowed sister who kept house for him.[4]

What sort of school was it over which James presided and Alington ruled? To ask the question begs several others. To begin with, could any Head Master of Eton be said to rule? Cyril Connolly who entered the school in 1918 and published the most readable account of his boyhood experiences in 1938 sets out there an ingenious allegory of the Etonian system of government.[5] According to this the Head Master was in the

4 Personal communication from Sir Robert Birley.
5 *Enemies of Promise* (1938) 233.

position of a medieval pope, the masters were the church and the boys in authority, the members of Pop, the Captain of the Boats and of the Eleven, the Captains of Houses, represented the feudal nobility. Certainly this is a plausible account of how direct disciplinary power impinged on the peasant, or ordinary boy. As an explanation of how the Head Master impressed himself, if he did impress himself, on the school it is also illuminating. His official contact with the boys except for those at the very top of the school and for delinquents charged with serious offences was largely indirect. Hence the importance and the value of entertaining them. Social life was not an optional extra but the axle on which the wheels turned.

In at least one other sense the medieval analogy is a fruitful one, namely that Eton was a plural society, not a monolithic or absolutist one sternly regulated by one coherent and consistent code. Napoleon would at once have abolished Eton if it had come within his purview. The question 'What was Eton like?' is not nonsensical but it is not capable of a single, uniform answer. It is so much a matter of groups and of individuals. Something at least can be done to establish who and what, at any given period, these were. Among the Collegers who had arrived at the school at about the same time as the new Provost and the new Head Master were George Orwell (Eric Blair) and Sir Roger Mynors: among Oppidans Sir Harold Acton and the future Lord Home. All the evidence suggests that Eton allowed these very different characters to develop with the luxuriant diversity that distinguished their subsequent careers: a pamphleteer, a scholar, an aesthete and a Prime Minister. Sir Harold Acton recalls in his memoirs his part in founding, towards the end of his time, the Eton Society of Arts. Its members included Robert Byron, Alan Clutton-Brock, Anthony Powell and Henry Green (Henry Yorke) 'who had started a novel called *Blindness* of which he never spoke ... This nursery of talent flourished so gaily that I have never been able to agree with the current platitude about our public schools standardizing character and suppressing originality ... The athletes resented our gaiety and feared our repartee. What right had we, who did not take their triumphs seriously, to our irrepressible exuberance? They vented their spite spasmodically ...'[6]

Eton, on this evidence, was propitious to individualism but it did not guarantee it. Repression and conformity are powerful instincts in any institution, particularly in those inhabited by boys. The cornerstone of Etonian liberties was having a room to oneself. Lord Home remembers at nearly sixty years distance the transition from his private school, Ludgrove, to Eton, in 1917:

'If Ludgrove was a shock, Eton was an earthquake. One House was as large as Ludgrove. The whole school numbered a thousand, and from the first week as a "fag" the new boy was in contact with the most senior boys. No preparation could adequately arm one for so dramatic a transition to independence, self-reliance and self-preservation within a largely self-governing structure.

'Each boy from the start had a room of his own, small but undeniably his territory, into which nobody, not even his House Master, could come without knocking.'[7]

Every system takes much of its colour from the people who administer it. Not all housemasters were as courteous or as scrupulous as Lord Home's. And boy-government where the housemaster was weak and the boys were vicious could be miserably tyrannical. But the possession of a room of one's own laid a foundation on which the tutorial system could build. From Cory onwards this had been the peculiar strength of Eton. No doubt to a number of boys these opportunities meant little or nothing. Happy in the common enjoyment of common things they passed through the school with the easy good humour they would have shewn in any establishment that provided the familiar and customary amenities of companionship, of the playing fields and the river. If few of them outside College took their work seriously few made themselves objectionable to those who did. Eton was large and liberal in a careless, off-hand, aristocratic way. If people wanted to spend

6 *Memoirs of an Aesthete* (1948), 91 – 3.
7 *The Way the Wind Blows*, 26.

their free time in acquiring the rudiments of scholarship or bird-watching or finding out about English watercolourists, well, let them. Always assuming of course that it did not conflict with some antecedent duty of an athletic nature.

Not all contemporary evidence supports this view. Henry Green's autobiography already referred to depicts Eton as a mean and servile place. Fear was the dominant emotion, toadying the prevalent mode of behaviour and success at games the standard of worth. The masters, 'a poor lot'[8], feebly connived at this childish and contemptible travesty of a liberal education. The moral effect was naturally deplorable, robbing the boys of candour, courage and manliness:

'We were feminine, not from perversion, although it is true that we were preoccupied by sex, but from a lack of any other kind of self-expression. Also we watched the effect we produced on others in the way women do, and this on account of the system under which the general opinion held of us had a disproportionate effect upon our security and in consequence upon our peace of mind. But whatever reasons we might have we screamed and shrieked rather than laughed and took a sly revenge rather than having it out with boxing gloves as parents will still imagine.'[9]

This autobiography carries conviction from its absence of self-righteousness. The author is indeed at pains to represent himself in the least flattering light. The tone of the book strangely echoes the Pauline self-abasement of seventeenth century puritanism: 'I was a chief, the chief, of sinners.' Since Henry Green's life and writings show a whole-hearted dislike of puritanism in any form this is certainly not a possible explanation. But it is difficult not to feel, particularly when reading the passage on snobbery,[10] that morbid self-depreciation has overwhelmed the author and submerged his subject matter. Such an impression is supported by a closer reading. 'I had passed ... out of the totalitarian state which is one's first year

8 *Pack my Bag*, 157.
9 *ibid* 113.
10 *ibid* 136 – 7.

or two at a public school, into a twilight of activity in which I was not so miserable because I had found friends of my own sort. We were allowed to form a Society of Arts. This point is a watershed, after this was no turning back. I determined to be a writer . . .'[11] Despite the sepulchral cadences it is a liberation that is here chronicled. And the support of kindred spirits, so fresh in the gratitude of Harold Acton, is at least acknowledged. That the book was written in a mood of deep depression is so manifest that Evelyn Waugh makes a sympathetic allusion to the fact in a private letter to its author.[12]

Green's dismissal of the masters as 'a poor lot' calls for some comments. His contemporary Lord Home dissents: ' . . .although many of the younger masters had fallen in the war, and many more were absent in the forces, the standard of teaching was high and given by some scholarly men'.[13] Among the temporary reinforcements of the staff were the historians C.R.L. Fletcher and J.M. Thompson and, in the modern languages department, Aldous Huxley. The first two were experienced university teachers of real brilliance and Huxley made up in intellectual distinction and fastidiousness of language for his miscasting as a schoolmaster. Sir Steven Runciman, then a boy in College, remembers 'Above all it was his use of words that entranced us. Eric Blair – the future George Orwell – who was my exact contemporary – would in particular make us note Aldous's phraseology. "That is a word we must remember" we used to say to each other . . . the taste for words and their accurate and significant use remained. We owe him a great debt for it.'[14] Among those boys whose literary taste he helped to form were Eddy Sackville-West and Lord David Cecil. He assisted Earl De La Warr, a boy who had embraced socialist opinions, in setting up the Political Society, a body run entirely by the boys, to which members of both Houses of Parliament and of every party were invited to speak and answer questions.[15]

11 *ibid*, 163.
12 *The Letters of Evelyn Waugh* (ed. Amory) (1980), 145.
13 *op. cit.* 27.
14 quot. Sybille Bedford *Aldous Huxley: a biography* (1973), i, 92.
15 *ibid*.

Most of these birds of passage had taken wing by the summer of 1919. But the regular masters who had remained at the school throughout the war included men of high intellectual quality and strong personality. Lord Home cites among the classicists A.S.F. Gow who returned in the middle twenties to a Fellowship at Trinity, Cambridge and C.M. Wells, a scholar whose passion for excellence extended into many fields. He had played both cricket and football for Cambridge and for England: his knowledge of wine inspired awe in circles where such matters are not taken lightly: his skill as a fly-fisherman earned him an obituary in *Salmon and Trout*. Its author, anxious to verify his references as so exact a scholar would have required, sent it to Wells' old colleague Gow, then well into his eighties. The obituary concluded with the words: 'As all his friends will remember, C.M. Wells was a great judge of claret, burgundy and port.' The draft was returned with the word 'burgundy' deleted.[16]

Among historians Lord Home remembers the teaching of G.W. Headlam and C.H.K. Marten. Headlam belonged to that school of Eton masters of which Oscar Browning and George Lyttelton were the great exemplars: lazy, brilliant and entertaining. Luxmoore and Cory may have criticised such men justly for their failure to train their pupils in habits of scholarship but they were adventurous and stimulating. Connolly in his generally dismissive treatment of the masters who taught him admits to having enjoyed, perhaps even to have profited from sitting under* Headlam. 'He brought commonsense and reasonable worldly values into his relations with boys ... he seemed to stand for tolerance, efficiency and a hatred of fuss.'[17] As to Henry Marten, who was to succeed Macnaghten as Vice-Provost in 1929 and Lord Quickswood as Provost in 1945, he occupied a unique place in the teaching of his subject, not just at Eton but in the public and grammar schools of his day. Warre had appointed him to teach history – the first master at Eton

16 Personal communication from Esmond Warner Esq.
 * The Etonian variant of this phrase is more active: 'being up to'.
17 *Enemies of Promise*, 285. F.M.H. Markham, the Oxford historian, told the present author that he found Headlam much the more valuable teacher of the two.

with this exclusive responsibility. Lyttelton, by remodelling the curriculum, had given him the opportunity of building it up as a specialist subject. His success in teaching boys and in picking colleagues soon made it one of the most important. The effect was felt in other schools and was reinforced by Marten's co-authorship with Townsend Warner, his opposite number at Harrow, of perhaps the most famous and widely circulated of all school history textbooks. It was natural that King George VI should choose him as historical tutor to the present Queen and her sister where, it is said, his absorption in his subject sometimes led him to address them as 'Gentlemen'.

'He was the first of my teachers,' writes Lord Home, 'to make me realize that the characters of history had once been human beings like us.' It was this gift of immediacy, of sympathetic imagination based on wide and deep learning that made his approach to history so fruitful and so stimulating. The advice he gave to Sir Robert Birley on appointing him to his staff is revealing of his own methods of teaching: Look up something to do with the period, it does not matter what, for ten minutes or so about half an hour before you are due to teach and then think about it as you walk to school.[18] It would be hard to think of a simpler or a subtler way of avoiding staleness.

Confirmation of Lord Home's judgment comes in unexpectedly emphatic terms from Connolly: 'Marten was a model of clarity and enthusiasm; he was the sanest of schoolmasters, but, for that reason, had less influence on us than a teacher like Headlam, who did not aspire to be impartial ... but only with Marten and Headlam did one get a feeling of shame; they were teachers whose rebukes of one boy enlisted against him the sympathy of the class ...'[19] Connolly says nothing of Gow, an interesting omission. Lord Home remembers not only the vivid and exciting teaching that made Greek his favourite dead language, but recalls his caustic wit and his collection of French Impressionists.[20] Since it is the burden of Connolly's criticism

18 Communication from Sir Robert Birley.
19 *Enemies of Promise* 285 – 6.
20 *op. cit.* 28.

of Eton that its aesthetic canon rejected anything that had any connexion with any modern European art or literature, it is strange that so conspicuous an exception should have escaped him. It is the stranger because of the fact that Gow was George Orwell's tutor, and Orwell, in his published writings dismissive of and even hostile to Eton, clearly retained an unbroken affection and respect for Gow from his boyhood to the last weeks of his life.[21] Connolly and Orwell were friends from their preparatory school days so vividly, some would say imaginatively, described in Orwell's *Such, such, were the joys*. In College Orwell was in the election immediately above. *Enemies of Promise* gives abundant evidence of subsequent discussion of persons and themes between two writers who had shared so much of their early experience. Why, then, is Gow not mentioned? Could he have been the master who wrote in his report 'Connolly has a vulgar streak?' There is other evidence that Connolly found it easier to frame criticism than to forgive it.

Two masters not mentioned by Lord Home earn particular commendation in *Enemies of Promise*. The French master de Satgé '... loved literature, and working with him, I apprehended that remoteness of great poetry from life which is inherent in the exaction of the form and creates literature, "la treille où le pampre à la rose s'allie" '.[22] No doubt the metaphor gains from being expressed in French (the reader may think that the whole passage would benefit from translation) but it is the same that Luxmoore used to justify the teaching of Latin verse composition. De Satgé is a weak link in the indictment of Eton outlined above. He lent his pupil *Limbo* and *Crome Yellow* and taught him to read such authors as Baudelaire, Verlaine and Mallarmé.[23]

The teacher to whom Connolly devotes far the most space is the one whom he evidently disliked and despised, while admitting his talents and even, narrow though the compass he allows them, his virtues. This was Hugh Macnaghten, who as Captain

21 see on this Stansky and Abrahams *The Unknown Orwell* (1972) passim.
22 *op. cit.* 289.
23 *ibid* 315.

of the School, it will be remembered, had dared to defy Warre's passionate zeal for the Corps, only to be captivated by the thrill of meeting Lord Roberts at dinner. What Connolly hated was Macnaghten's romanticism, a romanticism that, in his view, betrayed and defiled the beauties of the ancient authors, notably Homer and Virgil. Worse, it was deeply infused with sentimentality. Worse still it was combined with a Christianity that Connolly contemptuously rejected. And worst of all it came off. Connolly is exasperated into candour: 'Homer and Virgil were the pillars of an Eton education, it would be hard to get more pleasure then or now than we obtained from reading them.'[24] Once that concession is made, the objections to what Macnaghten and others read into them, however well founded, seem beside the point. It leads, in fact, to an uncharacteristic generosity:

'It may be wondered why I call Macnaghten a good teacher. The reason is that although he concentrated on moments of beauty, he did not neglect the encircling drudgery, and because, although his taste was uncertain, he would permit no blasphemy. To laugh at anything he thought good meant punishment. He chastened the hooligans ... and he insisted on the modesty, the abnegation without which great art cannot be appreciated. "Up" to him boys for the first time had the experience of literature and every now and then, in the dusty classrooms, grew aware of the presence of a god.'[25]

Two other masters, both subsequently known outside Eton, are mentioned by Connolly simply as instances of how money in the one case and birth in the other could earn a patronizing toleration from their snobbish, oafish pupils. These were John Christie, who later founded the Glyndebourne Opera, and George Lyttelton, whose correspondence with Sir Rupert Hart-Davis has delighted so many readers. John Christie was not, it must be admitted, a serious schoolmaster; but would the perfect school be wholly staffed by such? Lord Home's

24 *ibid* 278.
25 *ibid* (revised edition (1949) 219 – 220. The text of this passage in the first edition is unsatisfactory).

recollection of his ministrations shows that they had at least the merit of originality:

'His even odder father had left it in his will that John must adopt some profession in order to inherit his fortune, and when invalided out of the army he came to Eton as a master. His subject was science, although I suspect that this was never proved. I was "up" to him for Early School once a week for almost a year. The routine was this. He would appear late in a dressing-gown, distribute a book on "Levers" and then ring the bell for his butler. He would say to him "Childs, entertain the young gentlemen while I have my bath." By the time he had washed, and Childs had provided us with coffee and biscuits, John Christie was ready for a short dissertation on the magic of leverage. He never questioned us, which made us suspect that it was ground which was too dangerous for the teacher. Alas, it was too good to last. Childs' intelligence network had for once become rusty, and Christie overconfident, and the Head Master walked in unannounced. He took in the situation at a glance and that was the beginning of the end of John Christie's professional career.'[26]

George Lyttelton was the antithesis of Christie in everything but originality of mind and taste. As a boy at Eton he had won every distinction that the playing fields could offer and remained a revered authority on the most recondite points of the Field and the Wall Game. He had been in A.C. Benson's house and they had attained a completeness of sympathy that did not cloud their vision of each other. Benson summed up his feeling for him when, after being Captain of the House, he left to go up to Cambridge:

'... a great comfort – so strong, paternal, reasonable and truly loyal. It has been a great pleasure having him – though his mind is still flaccid and he is *very* indolent – almost incapable of hard pointed work. I am sure that his physical development is too pronounced. Though he is humorous and incisive in speech – but he neither reads or works, only moons.'

A few weeks later his care was amply rewarded:

26 *op. cit.* 30.

'One of the most affectionate and beautiful letters I have ever received from George Lyttelton: he says that he looked upon me really as a father ... says that I may have better pupils but never a more loving one. This is a letter of gold to me, and at this time ... Its outspokenness reveals its sincerity – and from a boy who is *not* given to sentiment.'[27]

Lyttelton returned to Eton as a master in 1908, succeeded to a house in 1924 and retired in 1945 (the last, incidentally, of the proprietary housemasters. After him housemasters rented their houses from the school, but could still choose how well or ill to feed their boys and to minister to their comforts. Under the modern system housemasters receive an increase in salary and various other benefits but make no direct profit). The tradition of cultivating the individual taste was worthily represented in his teaching. It flowered with his introduction of English Literature as an optional subject into the curriculum in 1925 (he had taught it as an unofficial extra study from much earlier). The roll-call of authors who gratefully own their debt to his stimulus and to his encouragement is a long one. John Verney, Bernard Fergusson, Peter and Ian Fleming, John Bayley, Sir Rupert Hart-Davis himself: this is but a sampling.

The great quality of George Lyttelton's mind was, as A.C. Benson had divined, its indolence. He was not in any hurry to arrive, had indeed no discernible objective in mind and was apparently entirely without ambition. This freedom from the habitual preoccupations of the adult and the scholar left him ready to observe minutely and accurately the eccentricities of human behaviour and the idiosyncrasies of character that he came across in his reading and in his experience of life. He brought the same leisurely literate fastidiousness to the pavilion at Lords as he did to whatever ancient or modern author he happened to be teaching, or reading for his own amusement. Disraeli's advice 'Read no history, nothing but biography: for that is life without theory' is frowned on for its frivolity by the reigning school of historians. But anyone who has ever had to teach history to boys and girls will recognise that it contains the

27 MS Journal, ix, 44 – 5; x, 17.

essential truth that Lord Home identified in Henry Marten's approach to the subject. The same might be said about George Lyttelton's power to make literature an extension and not an obstruction to real life. He was also gifted with an ear and a voice that made it impossible for his pupils to remain wholly insensitive to the beauties of language and the nuances of phrase. Much of this can be perceived or guessed by those who know him only through the letters of his old age, exchanged weekly with Sir Rupert Hart-Davis. His humour and his inexhaustible range of anecdote, always pithy, generally unexpected and rarely malicious, is also evident there. So, too, are the strength of his prejudices, the limitations of his imaginative sympathy and the vagaries of his taste. That anyone who cares for good writing could look down his nose at both Jane Austen and George Orwell is surprising: but we have the evidence of this correspondence to show that both participants did. Not to admire what all the world has agreed to admire is a reassurance of individuality particularly valuable in a teacher. George Lyttelton encouraged his pupils to form their own opinions.

This by no means exhausts the list of remarkable teachers to be found at Eton at the beginning of the Alington-James epoch but to press the point further would exhaust the reader. Henry Green's assertion that the masters were 'a poor lot' does not stand up well to examination His charges of snobbery and effeminacy must be matter for another chapter. But perhaps the more widely held view that the Eton of this period was homosexual by aspiration if not by practice demands precedence.

CHAPTER EIGHT

Love and Friendship

HOMOSEXUALITY IS A TOPIC envenomed by past injustice and flattened by present consensus. In the indifference which now enshrouds the world of sexual morals an attempt has been made to revivify this particular aspect by hijacking one of the most attractive and one of the few irreplaceable adjectives in the English language. Even that daring and certainly immoral expedient has failed to rescue the subject. Boredom seems its inevitable attendant. Yet everyone who has not been at a public school and many who have believe it to be, like garlic in Mediterranean cookery, the ubiquitous and inescapable ingredient of these institutions.

In a society that from the accidents of its origin or purpose happened to consist of a single sex, the armed forces, the colleges of Oxford and Cambridge, the public schools as they were up to and beyond the war of 1939–45, homosexuality was obviously and always an inherent possibility. To what degree it was tolerated or punished was a matter more of tradition, discipline and acceptability than of morality. Law defined and prohibited, as with persons of school age it still does, certain homosexual acts. But it had and has nothing to say about the atmosphere, the climate, the ambience. Anecdotes of Eton as of every public school are rich in the embarrassed unintelligibilities of housemasters tackling this difficult subject, frequently rendered yet more impenetrable by confusing it with preparation for being confirmed. The confusion was often shared by the recipient of these mysterious utterances. Adolescent sexuality is rarely straighforward in its orientation. But it sometimes is, and in a school as large as Eton there are always likely to be boys whose awakening desires are directed towards their own sex. What was the attitude of the authorities and of Etonian public opinion towards such manifestations? Was it influenced by the pull of the ancient authors, many of them strongly homosexual in sentiment, or by the push of a Christianity much sterner and less compromising in its condemnation then than now? Was the ethos of Eton sympathetic or secretly encouraging where it could not openly approve?

Cyril Connolly in an interesting analysis of the essentials of Etonian culture in his time focuses attention on Plato. 'Platonism was everywhere, popping up in sermons and Sunday questions, in allusions to Neoplatonism, in essays by Dean Inge, at the headmaster's dinner-parties, or in my tutor's pupil-room ... For there was no doubt that homosexuality formed an ingredient in this ancient wisdom. It was one forbidden tree round which our little Eden dizzily revolved. In a teaching conscious, and somewhat decadently conscious, of beauty, its presence in the classics was taken for granted; it was implicit in Plato's humour and aesthetic. Yet Eton, like all public schools, had no solution for sex ...

'The result was that boys learnt to walk a tightrope; the sentimental friendship was permitted in some houses and forbidden in others, allowed to some boys and denied to their fellows, or permitted and then suppressed according to the changing views and vigilance of the housemaster. No one could be sure on what ground they trod ... One thing was certain, the potentially homosexual boy was the one who benefited, whose love of beauty was stimulated, whose appreciation was widened, and whose critical powers were developed; the normal boy, free from adolescent fevers, missed both the perils and the prizes; he was apt to find himself left out.'[1]

It has to be remembered that *Enemies of Promise* is the first and most distinguished of its author's many apologies for his failure to achieve his ambitions as an original writer. That his talents as a parodist, a critic and an essayist might to some degree

1 *op. cit.* 280 – 1.

disable him as a poet or a novelist is not admitted. Eton was to blame. With her siren voices, her poise, her cultivation, her beauty, she had seduced the young swain who else had known to sing and build the lofty rhyme. Decadent, sickly and sentimental as she really was she could work her wicked magic only on those whose own perceptions and sensibilities exposed them to her subtle poisons. 'The normal boy, free from adolescent fevers' was safe. But what reason is there for thinking that normal boys are free from adolescent fevers? Surely the contrary is to be presumed. And what is the author's warrant for the contrast drawn in this passage between the normal and the potentially homosexual? The conclusion may seem forced: but the insight and observation that precede if they do not support it, command attention. Few who were at Eton in Connolly's time and after would dissent from the view that much depended on the views and vigilance of the individual housemaster.

'I see Cattley is dead' wrote Rupert Hart-Davis to George Lyttelton in 1958. 'I never knew him to speak to, but didn't much like what I heard about him ... I'm sure he was a suppressed paederast ... how say you?' 'You are quite right' replied Cattley's old friend and colleague, like many bachelor beaks ... many of them excellent beaks ... he was a sublimated homosexual, the adjective, or rather participle, being just as certain as the noun. He was perhaps a little too frank in his preference for bright boys of fourteen to all boys, bright or not, of eighteen.'[2] None the less it was maliciously rumoured to be his practice, startling to modern ears and strange then, to kiss all his boys, even the eighteen-year-olds, goodnight when he went round the house.[3] Ian Fleming's housemaster used to insist on inspecting the whole house in a state of nakedness at regular intervals. The alleged purpose was to make sure that they had not contracted venereal disease. Other motives naturally suggested themselves. The creator of James Bond perhaps owed something to this early introduction to sexual fantasy.

[2] Lyttelton – Hart-Davis Letters, iii, 108 – 110.
[3] An old boy of his has, however, recently told me that this was, in his time at least, an exaggeration, though one had to take care to avoid an encircling arm.

Such conduct was of course unusual and did not fall within George Lyttelton's carefully qualified definition. It was one which his old housemaster, A.C. Benson, would have entirely approved. Benson's biographer, David Newsome, himself a don and a headmaster, expounds the matter with a wisdom and a clarity that leaves little more to say. Since his treatment of the subject reaches back to Benson's hero, William Johnson Cory, and stretches forward to the period when George Lyttelton was himself a housemaster it is perhaps permissible to quote it at some length.

'Love is a noble passion; and no less noble for being the bond which may unite two persons of the same sex or of different ages. Such love might, at certain stages of history and civilisation, be considered unconventional, but in itself it is neither unnatural or immoral. Indeed the propensity to feel such a love, in a schoolmaster or a don, can often be the particular gift which he brings to his calling; and if such emotions were branded as ignoble or base, then it would remove from these professions the inner commitment or vocation which so often inspires them.'[4]

Benson was well aware that physical beauty in boys could attract him romantically as it never could in the opposite sex: or rather, as Dr Newsome points out, in so far as it did it was just because the girl in question had a boyish charm. But romance was for him the very antithesis of lust or even desire. It meant in life what it meant in literature: a wind that brushed the cheek of the spirit, a haunting, evanescent loveliness that fled from the approach of physical possession. Benson remained chaste throughout his life, notwithstanding his early emancipation from dogmatic Christianity and his growing scepticism of convention. It was not that he thought homosexual intimacies wrong (though he certainly would have condemned a master who practised or permitted them as false to his trust) it was that he found even the thought of them repulsive. Dr Newsome quotes a conversation that Benson had at the very end of his life with his brother, Fred:

4 *On the edge of Paradise*, 195.

'We discussed the homo sexual question [*sic*. the word was hardly a generation old]. It does seem to me out of joint that marriage should be a sort of virtuous duty, honourable, beautiful and praiseworthy – but that all irregular sexual expression should be bestial and unmentionable. The 'concurrence of the soul' is the test surely?'[5]

Benson was fastidious and intensely self-critical. To clear his mind of cant, to avoid sloppiness and muddle in forming moral judgments, was his first concern. He was struck, as Cyril Connolly was, by the unreasonableness of steeping intelligent young minds in Greek poetry and philosophy and expecting them to remain impervious to its often insistent homosexuality. 'Isn't it really rather dangerous to let boys read Plato if one is desirous that they should accept conventional moralities?' Cory had accepted the dilemma and had reflected it in his poetry. But Cory, though as swift, if not swifter, to recoil from the grossness of carnal relations, was more passionate in his affections. His attachments to boys who combined purity of heart, generosity of spirit with the tender, wildrose beauty of youth were more consuming and more open. Indeed among the many things that Benson admired in Cory it was to this that he recurred:

'What is the attractive thing about W. J. [Cory]? It is, I think, that with a perfectly furnished mind, strong, virile, self-possessed and liberal, he yet deliberately put the intellect far behind the affections. Hence comes the coolness and depth of his poetry – the romance, the heart-hunger, the eye for beauty (in character and in the few, outward avenues of perception nature allowed him) – the tenderness.'[6]

It was this that had led, one way or another, to the summary, ignominious dismissal of the greatest of Eton masters, the richest, most creative individual influence in the formation of the tradition already described. But *what* way? Cory's disgrace rears up again and again because its cause has never been officially divulged. His attachments led him into writing letters that

5 *ibid.*
6 *ibid*, 80.

expressed the ardour of his nature and the intensity of his affections. A parent might have taken alarm; might even have concluded that his son was being seduced. But was this inference proved? This question is not a prurient raking among the embers of a long forgotten scandal. It is crucial to the understanding of Eton's standards in these matters. If the imputation was known to be true then the masters who regarded Cory's treatment as harsh were saying in effect that a member of the staff should not be dismissed for having homosexual relations with a boy. Such a position seems hardly credible in such an institution. Yet rumour has freely asserted, and continues to assert, that Cory had such an affair. The terms in which he wrote to the future Lord Rosebery, a favourite pupil, echo the literary conventions of the distracted lover.

> My dear Dalmeny.
>
> What is the matter?
>
> Wood says you say you are not coming here any more, because I cut you.
>
> I don't agree to that.
>
> You cut me for four days.
>
> You came here on Thursday night and I was very polite, only Mr Day's presence prevented any ordinary conversation.
>
> On Friday night I made reasonable overtures, stomaching my pride, which is not less than yours: only reason convinces me that it must be subdued, or else I shall lose more than I can afford to lose in this dearth of sympathy ...
>
> Come and have it out, if you have any grievance.
>
> I have been unhappy for a week without you, though too proud to say so ...[7]

The recipient of this letter had gone up to Oxford in 1866, six years before Cory's sudden departure. Another pupil perhaps as high in his affections was the future *éminence grise* of Edwardian England, the second Lord Esher. But he left Eton in 1870. Both men were widely reputed to be homosexuals, so

---

7 The full text of this letter is printed in Robert Rhodes James *Rosebery*, p. 37.

that rumour and speculation have found encouragement that the mere facts of chronology clearly contradict. Whatever gave Hornby the pretext for dismissing Cory, they can have had nothing to do with it. Yet if Cory wrote to boys in these terms an intercepted letter would offer his enemies their chance. Even A.C. Benson was himself baffled in his efforts to find out the truth but apparently concluded that Cory's dismissal was justified. His friend Warre Cornish, one of several masters who had admired Cory as a colleague and had kept up with him after he left Eton 'could tell, or chose to tell, very little. Any more writing, he said, "would only stir the wasps who sit upon his tomb." '[8]

Everything about Cory – and most conspicuously the tone of his poetry – suggests in idea of courtly love whose poignancy derives from the very impossibility of its consummation. He was a romantic whose romanticism had gained in thrust from being compressed within the discipline of Greek and Latin. As Benson so clearly saw, his romanticism was the conscious choice of a powerful and analytic intellect, not the emotional self-indulgence of a Marianne Dashwood. Morally, intellectually and physically Cory was fastidious and kept himself in hard training. His contempt, distaste and dislike for those who surrendered themselves, like his old pupil and colleague Oscar Browning, to ease and luxury bristle from his letters and journals. In the absence of evidence to support the rumours, themselves easily explicable on the grounds of his treatment by the Eton authorities, the presumption must surely be that he stands at the head of the category defined by George Lyttelton. In that line of succession stand, certainly, Benson and Hugh Macnaghten, whose teaching extorted Connolly's unwilling admiration. Others inconspicuously suggest themselves: Luxmoore for example. None of these men (it must be repeated because it is better to be tedious than to misrepresent) condoned, still less approved, homosexual conduct or seemed by their words and actions to imply that they did so. But Dr Newsome's point that the boarding schools and resident universities of the era of

8 *ibid.*

127

axiomatic sexual segregation gained much from the particular affections of such men demands acknowlegment.

Not all masters, still less all boys, lived by the standards of the men whose names have been mentioned in this chapter. The cult of athleticism, venerated by some masters in the twenties and thirties to the exclusion of virtually everything else, the narcissism of Pop*, that touched its heights in Denys Finch Hatton, who superadded spongebag trousers to the already glorious raiment of the Eton Society, may have stimulated homosexual propensities. Beating and flogging excited darker passions. A house where the master, caring only about games, left spoilt and arrogant young men with more or less unlimited power over thirty of their juniors could be a horrible place. It was not only the pain and the fear and the humiliation of corporal punishment capriciously and sometimes brutally inflicted. It was, scaled down to the world of the schoolboy and thus mercifully limited in time and space, the nightmare atmosphere of the police state. The Library, as the small self co-opting body in charge of the house was called, had the powers of the police, the judiciary and the Home Secretary combined and extended, in theory, to infinity. If the housemaster were weak, lazy or sycophantic or if in his anxiety to assert himself he antagonized his Library it was a poor look-out for his boys. An open scandal could give the Head Master the opportunity of putting things to rights by sacking the boys who had misused their position and, in extreme cases, taking the house away from the master to whom it had been entrusted. Obviously it was preferable to anticipate such a catastrophe. Not until Elliott's appointment in 1933 was the Head Master empowered, indeed enjoined, to exercise a right of selection as to which members of his staff might succeed to a vacant housemastership. Hornby, Warre, Lyttelton and Alington had had no choice in the matter. Before their time, as we have seen, the privilege was jealously reserved to the classical tutors: but it had been a privilege enjoyed as of right, not dependent on the Head Master's approval. The only barrier was religious conformity, since preparation for confirmation

* see p. 147.

was regarded as one of the most important of a housemaster's functions. A Roman Catholic was therefore disqualified. In 1930 William Hope-Jones, a housemaster in my time, had corresponded anxiously with Alington when he began to think of becoming a Quaker. The Head Master, no friend to doctrinal zealotry, raised no objection.[9] One can imagine the glittering acerbities that such an inquiry might have elicited had it been addressed a few years later to Lord Hugh Cecil.

In 1933 Elliott was told by the Governing Body that his first task would be to inform four masters that they would not succeed to houses. Various compensations were offered to them in the way of money and status.[10] An important precedent had been set. From that point succession to a house was no longer automatic. Both Alington and Elliott have been generally admired for their tact and judgment of men. But undoubtedly some very unsuitable people held houses during their time. Once in, a housemaster could hardly be turned out until the Head Master had some solid evidence of his incapacity. The devolution of responsibility to the housemaster and the delegation of administrative power to the boys made this often very difficult to obtain. Everyone might know that so-and-so's was a sink of iniquity without being able to prove it. In public schools as in the underworld to inform was taboo.

Thanks to the vigilance and shrewdness of the Head Masters bad houses were not common but they were not unknown. Homosexuality was a feature of them, perhaps because like bullying, or drinking, it was a form of licentiousness. Had the school been co-educational no doubt vanity and appetite would in many cases have sought an outlet in the opposite sex. Drugs were unknown to the adolescents of the twenties and thirties but had this not been the case no doubt they would have contended with drink for the primacy in fashionable vices. If bad houses were uncommon, houses that left a great deal to be desired were not rare. What was seen at its most obvious in a bad house was in them more muted. Houses ranged through the

9 William Hope-Jones. *A Memoir*. (Privately published, n.d.) 38 ff.
10 Private information.

spectrum of quality. They were individual organisms and, being individual, they differed not only from each other but from themselves. They grew better or worse, more obsessed with football or more interested in music, more liberal or more stodgy, more or less apt to be homosexual.

The inbuilt forces that made for this last tendency may thus briefly be summarized. First and most fundamental the single sex character of the institution and the age of its inmates. Second the cult of games, often promoted by the masters, which added a touch of the numinous and more than a touch of the romantic to the physical beauty, the grace of movement and elegance of form so common in young athletes. Third the enhancing of this by the trappings of success at games, colours, caps, blazers, exquisitely pressed white flannels and the rest of it. Fourth the Nirvana of the Eton Society or Pop, who combined the ultimate in dandyism with the absolute in power. Fifth, applying only to those who could read Greek authors easily or were curious enough to read them in translation, the ethos of Athens in the fifth century B.C.

Whether this last exerted an active influence may be doubted. To argue that familiarity with the literature of a homosexual civilization predisposes the reader to homosexual practices belongs to the same order of reasoning as that ridiculed by Johnson's 'Who drives fat oxen should himself be fat.' Successive Royal Commissions on censorship and obscenity have failed to establish any satisfactory relation of cause and effect between what a man reads and what he does. If it be argued that men are one thing and boys another, a more marked tendency towards homosexuality should reveal itself among the classical specialists than among the mathematicians or historians. There appears to be no evidence whatever that this is in fact the case, or if there is no one has yet cited it. What Cory and Benson and others have contended is that the assumptions of the ancient authors are irreconcilable with the official morality and discipline of English public schools in the nineteenth and twentieth centuries and that intelligent boys would perceive this. What Connolly added was the titillation, all but irresistible to a literary journalist of the late thirties, of proclaiming decadence and corruption in high places and imputing it at least partially and by insinuation to the homosexuality evident in classical authors and latent in some of the men who taught them.

If there were fashionable and intellectual forces making for homosexuality in the Eton of the twenties they were to be looked for in more advanced circles. The aesthetes who found in Harold Acton a champion against the religion of games and other pious conventionalities were eager to flaunt the manners and tastes that the athletes would condemn as effeminate. Partly this was instinctive defiance. Partly it arose from a desire to be daring and up-to-the-minute: so many of the admired figures in the arts and letters of the twenties were known to be homosexual, and, conversely, so closed were the disapproving ranks of the Old Guard, even where its members were secretly so inclined. And finally some of these boys were homosexual. One of them, Brian Howard, was to be parodied in one of Connolly's most celebrated performances 'Where Engels Fears to Tread'. The same self-conscious preciosity there so brilliantly captured is apparent in the Journal, now in the School Library at Eton, that he kept as a boy during the year 1921.

21 January	... I have a nice new room ... I order papers (Daily Telegraph, Athenaeum, New Age etc etc). A new wastepaper basket comes from Selfridges. Writing paper from Harrods. I write a post card to Mum.
22 January	I also write Mummy a letter. Mr Putnam measures my room for the new cretonne (? chintz). Also I order the 'English Review' at Spottiswoodes [the Eton stationery and book shop]. My food (jam, cakes, sweets etc etc) comes from the Army and Navy.
	P.S. William [Acton] presents me with a charming tiny reproduction of Bronzino. I also have a talk with Harold.
23 January *(Sunday)*	During the day I do my Sunday Questions well, and read a little Kipling.
	I receive a letter from Mummy and write her one. Harold [Acton] sees me and I visit him.

	He gives me the catalogue of the Third International [? Photographic Exhibition]. Charming of him.
25 January	Mother comes down at 2.30 and we spend till nearly 4 o'clock tidying and re-arranging the room... She brings down my books and the 26 yards of stuff (blue-white-brown chintz).
	We settle to have the room re-papered next holidays.
2 February	I am very pleased with the chintz.
4 February	I write an amusing incoherency for fun when my work was finished (dada).
5 February	I polish off some Dadaistic poems and send them to Edith Sitwell.
15 February	In the morning I received a *wonderful* letter from Edith Sitwell. She encloses me back my poems but compliments me tremendously and writes four pages advising me and asking for more and other poems. I *am* so encouraged.

There is, of course, nothing remotely homosexual in the passages quoted. Yet they express exactly the image of the Etonian pansy: exquisite, expensive, Sybaritic and arrogant if not altogether without an engaging enthusiasm and an obvious enjoyment of life. The author was, as an adult, an active and open homosexual so that he may be presumed to have been so inclined in his adolescence.

Does it, in any case, matter? It is clear from the diary that what really excited the boy were his literary and artistic ambitions. These were crowned by his publication in the following year of a handsome quarto, *The Eton Candle*. Brian Howard's introductory article on the New Poetry is tedious, pretentious stuff. But he had gathered a distinguished list of Old Etonian contributors including Gerald Kelly (to become in 1930 the school's first Royal Academician), Osbert and Sacheverell Sitwell, Aldous Huxley, Maurice Baring, Harold and William Acton and Anthony Powell, making his debut as a draughtsman not as a writer. No one except an inquirer into the history of Eton in the twenties would wish to read it. But if it now lies stranded, a weathered curiosity of vanity publishing, it must have made a brave show at its launching.

It is this tang of the open sea, that ocean sailed by writers of the *avant garde*, that *The Eton Candle* brought to the sluggishness of the Thames Valley. It spotlighted the aesthetes and their manner of life, polarising by an easy association of thought homosexuality and modern art at one end and heterosexuality and football at the other. There was of course no real warrant for such a correspondence. But it helps to explain the excited suggestion of decadence and subversion that touches even Connolly's treatment of the subject. Homosexuality among adolescents is as old as the hills. What changes is fashion and emphasis in morality and discipline.

The twenties and the thirties saw the ebbing of a tide that had started to run strongly in the late nineteenth century. Keate and his contemporaries for all their simple faith in flogging as an essential part of education do not seem to have found in homosexual activities its obvious and ready justification. Professor Honey in his excellent new history of the public schools in the nineteenth century dates this sudden concern with what can hardly have been a new problem to the 1880s.[11] In 1881 the Headmaster of Clifton chose as the theme for his Presidential Address to the Education Society 'Morality in Public Schools'. Briefly he argued that moral instability and physical decrepitude were the terrible consequences of adolescent sexual activity in its traditional forms. This was enthusiastically taken up in journals and newspapers. Amid the hubbub it is refreshing to hear the cool, civilized commonsense of an Old Etonian whose letter Professor Honey prints at length. He admits that sexual immorality was rife in the Eton of his time. 'I have in my mind's eye a list – a long one, I regret to say – of those who at my school were unfortunately conspicuous . . . in this particular manner.' But he denies utterly the conclusions so alarmingly drawn and so readily accepted. '. . . Those very boys have become Cabinet Ministers, statesmen, officers, clergymen, country gentlemen etc . . . they are nearly all of them fathers of

11 J.R. de S. Honey *Tom Brown's Universe* (1977), 179 ff.

thriving families, respected and prosperous ... The moral to be pointed is, that happily an evil so difficult to cure is not so disastrous in its results. How many boys, or rather men, can Mr Wilson [the Headmaster of Clifton] point to who owe their ruin to the immorality he talks of?'

This is the authentic Etonian note, so irritating to the zealot, of the man of the world and of the aristocrat. Pragmatic and slightly disdainful it suggests that it would be a good idea to look at the world as it really is, and not to make a fuss about things that don't in the end matter. It reflects the attitude that prevailed in the school in the late thirties and lies at the heart of that most Etonian *roman fleuve* Anthony Powell's *A Dance to the Music of Time*. Bound up with the whole history of Eton the influence of aristocracy demands examination.

CHAPTER NINE

———•◊•———

The Aristocratic Inheritance

NOWHERE IS THE ENGLISH PREFERENCE for avoiding sharp cut straight lines more evident than in contemporary attitudes towards aristocracy. Few would use the word in conversation with strangers. Indeed to talk about it at all is to risk being thought snobbish or reactionary or eccentric, if not all three. The characteristics of the satirical stereotype are apt to be transferred from the subject to the person who raises it. This inhibition like the Victorian limitations on what might be discussed in polite society heightens the interest of the topic. The details and circumstances of aristocratic life fascinate and excite the more because they exude an aura of illicit pleasure. Some of the most admired English novelists of the mid-twentieth century, Evelyn Waugh, Anthony Powell, Nancy Mitford, have chosen aristocratic themes and subjects for their art and it is to be doubted that they have lost readers by doing so. Where the novelists have led the television script writers have followed. Aristocracy may be an improper subject for general conversation but it is not an exploded idea or an outmoded phenomenon.

The English idea of aristocracy is hazier than that prevailing on the continent. There it is simply a question of pedigree. Either one is *geboren* or one is not. Unless there have been scandals or infidelities the fact can be easily established by consulting the appropriate reference books. Essentially the European notion of aristocracy is that of a caste system rather than of a class. In continental eyes the English nobility hardly qualify. Peerages are created without reference to blood and breeding, scions of ancient families pair off with dairymaids or chorus girls. Banking and brewing replenish the dwindling reserves of the landed families. This may be socially, politically and economically advantageous but that is neither here nor there. To the true believer, aristocracy in the clear, narrow, sense of pure genealogy exists as an end in itself. Indeed in the Austro-Hungarian Empire it was the practice, even as late as 1914, to exempt the young heirs to great names from military service, or at least from any that was likely to expose them to serious risks.[1]

Such a notion, perfectly logical on the grounds of preserving a rare and supremely valuable species, is repellent to those who found their idea of aristocracy on the older concept, embodied in the feudal system, of the right and duty of leadership in war. That, historically, is what kings and nobles are for. Yet already by the seventeenth century it was widely recognised that the disadvantages of exposing the sovereign or his heir to the hazards of battle might well outweigh the inspiration of personal example. In England the principle established itself during the reign of Charles II who did not himself take the field against a foreign enemy and forbade his brother James, an admired military and naval commander, to expose himself further after a narrow escape in his first and only fleet action against the Dutch. The only two kings who subsequently chose to lead their troops in person, William III and George II, were both foreigners, educated in a different political tradition. But this convention never extended itself downwards into the aristocracy. On the contrary, the presumption was that birth qualified a man for command. Even Pepys who introduced the first professional examination for naval officers did not doubt that good breeding was in itself a recommendation. He simply wished to ensure that those who possessed it were also technically competent.

All this may seem to have nothing to do with Eton. But the idea of aristocracy, the reasons why it was in the past so unquestioningly accepted and why it is now approached, so to speak,

---

1 see on all this Cecilia Sternberg, *The Journey* (1978) *passim*.

on tiptoe are prerequisite to any understanding of the place. The first essential is to distinguish between the uses of a word in which abstract and concrete alternate at whim. Aristocracy is, or certainly has been, admired as an ideal, expressed in a number of familiar maxims, *noblesse oblige*, the post of honour is the post of danger, and so on. Loneliness and grandeur lie at the heart of it. It knows nothing of competitiveness on the one hand or of the team spirit on the other. It is an extreme expression of individuality, an intemperate, reckless assertion of freedom. 'Liberty,' Sir Lewis Namier wrote, 'in its very nature, is an aristocratic or oligarchic attribute, possessed by single trees spreading above a lawn rather than by trees in a forest.'[2] Above all it is the negation of pettiness, of self-interest, of calculation. The aristocrat is too sure of himself and what he stands for to bother about what other people think of him, too far above the sordid necessities of life to seek promotion or reward. He does not have to think about climbing because he is already at the top.

This adumbration of the idea shows some of its attractions and suggests some of its drawbacks. But the word is also, and much more often, used to describe a body of people easily identifiable to outsiders as well as to themselves. The basis of this identification is genealogical but such credentials are not too closely scrutinised, except by experts. What counts, what always has counted in England, is style of life. To live like an aristocrat for a couple of generations is to be one. This of course presupposes the existence of aristocrats for the aspirant to imitate. As in the making of whisky or sherry the new wines are added to a vat in whose depths lurk older liquors. Blending is the art of English society.

In this process of assimilation Eton has had a large share. It is often asserted that the proliferation of public schools in the nineteenth century answered the need of the newly rich to launder the money from shops and factories and enable their sons to slip inconspicuously into the ranks of the gentry. But Eton, though she rode the crest of the Victorian boom, is to be

2 *Conflicts* (1942), 188.

measured on a different historical scale. From the beginning the school had been in the orbit of king and court; from the beginning College had provided an opportunity for boys who were neither rich nor well-born. In the centuries when distinctions of rank were accepted as an unalterable part of the scheme of things these were reflected at Eton. The Commensals who had been part of the original foundation disappeared after the Civil War. But they were succeeded by noblemen who lived in their own lodgings under the supervision of private tutors and enjoyed other privileges. 'The day of breaking up is the sixteenth of December' wrote the young Lord Hastings to his father the Earl of Huntingdon in 1690, 'the noblemen commonly go away the day before because of the crowd ...'[3] Until College was reformed in the early Victorian period a considerable proportion of its intake came from the sons of local tradesmen who were prepared to undergo the rigours of life there. Some of them entered the school as Oppidans. There was always therefore a breadth of class structure surprising in a school generally assumed to be exclusive by nature. Did the tradesmen's sons and the noblemen's sons mix or keep themselves distinct? The answer would seem to be that there was a degree of assimilation. Friendships were formed, cemented in later life by the patronage, especially in presentations to church livings, which landed families had at their disposal.[4] But it was for families who had risen from modest origins to great wealth that Eton smoothed a path. Sir Stephen Fox who rose from being a clerk in the royal household to the lucrative office of Paymaster General sent his younger son Henry there. Henry, an even more successful politician than his father, sent his son Charles James to the school. So well established had the Foxes become in so short a time that Charles who had been spoilt and indulged by his father was held by many to have altered the whole tone of Eton by setting a fashion for luxury and expense from which it took long to recover.

3 *Etoniana* 57/107.
4 see for some interesting examples of this 'The Rise of the Professional Class: An Eton Microcosm' in A.R. Wagner *Pedigree and Progress* (1975), especially pp. 129 – 131.

Was Charles James Fox an aristocrat? If he set fashions that his aristocratic contemporaries followed, if he was accepted by them not only as an equal but as a leader, if he shared their amusements, their manners, their style, the answer must surely be yes. Acceptance not pedigree is the test. And the openness, the fluidity of English society, preferable as we may think it to the hierarchical rigidity of the foreigners, does not make it any less snobbish. An eighteenth century Head Master such as Dr Foster, who was the son of a Windsor tradesman, or his successor Dr Davies, who was nicknamed 'Barber', did not find their origins forgotten. Both men were too harsh in exerting authority, a common symptom of insufficient self-confidence, and both provoked rebellions. It was not their lineage but their style that was resented and, because it was resented, ridiculed as socially inferior. English snobbery is based more on manners than on extraction. There are, of course, notable exceptions. Some people seek familiarity with noblemen however dull or unattractive simply because they are noblemen. In the eighteenth and even the nineteenth century there were other obvious inducements. The nobility were rich and powerful: their protection was one of the greatest advantages that an ambitious man could possess. But that is careerism, not snobbery. It is not in practice always easy to say where the one ends and the other begins but they are essentially distinct.

The weight of opinion among those who have been at Eton as boys or masters is that it is not a snobbish place. Even so sharp a critic as A.C. Benson is emphatic on the point: 'The one mercy of Eton is that so large a percentage of boys are sons of rich and "important" people that the ordinary snobbishness of schools simply doesn't come in, and a boy has to make his own position by activity, cheerfulness and kindness.'[5] More comprehensive is the assertion of Alington, himself the first non-Etonian Head Master since the time of Charles II writing to another non-Etonian, Lionel Smith, whom he was urging to succeed him: 'My great difficulty always is (when appointing masters) to convince people of what is really true that this is the

5 *Etoniana* 103/43, 20 June 1898.

least exclusive and least narrow place of education in the country.'[6] These words go far to define the attraction of aristocracy which essentially consists in lack of constraint. It is the freedom, the ease, of people who are perfectly assured and perfectly mannered that makes their company so agreeable and so exhilarating to the clever and the articulate. Of course there are in real life aristocrats who are tyrannical, boorish, dotty or tiresome in some way or other just as there are Frenchmen who do not care about food: but both are atypical, unrepresentative of the special qualities, good, bad or morally indifferent, by which their categories are identified. All the great Eton figures from Cory down to M.R. James were susceptible to this charm, aware that they were, and grateful for it. The coolness, the absence of fuss, the easy manners that characterise aristocracy are specially valuable to the scholar and the teacher as counter-weights to his own obsessions. Scholarship involves passion and in particular passion for detail. A teacher must stimulate, must provoke and must find himself willy-nilly a disciplinarian. Education in the sense of a training in scholarship and the rules of argument is, we are repeatedly told by the Young Turks of the left, in itself bourgeois. Certainly its practitioners would fit more easily into this classification than any other. Perhaps it is this perception expressed with a more elegant fancy that A.C. Benson was hinting at in the passage quoted on p.93. The order at which education aims is the result of effort and of discipline, the cardinal virtues of the middle class. The bewitchments of aristocratic society lie in its effortlessness and spontaneity. The mixing of these two traditions has been valuable not only for Eton but for the country. It was certainly if impalpably present in the atmosphere of the place between the wars. Obviously it favoured the liberality, the resistance to conformity, that has been so persistent an element in its character.

That it also favoured snobbery has been the view of some who knew the place during this period. Henry Green's autobiography already cited certainly supports this. But it is not easy to disentangle what the author is saying about himself in

6 MS letter dated 8 May 1933 in the possession of Edward Hodgkin Esq.

what was evidently a state of acute depression from what is a dispassionate recollection of Eton about 1920.[7] A less ambiguous indictment is to be found in *Decent Fellows* (1930), a deservedly forgotten novel that enjoyed a brief *succès de scandale* because its author[8] was an Etonian and the son of a housemaster. Accurate in trivialities of school organization and custom, the book carries no conviction in characterization, incident or dialogue. The *Eton College Chronicle* concluded its review (was it perhaps written by George Lyttelton?) 'To the worm the world must appear all mud.' A week or two later the ex-Captain of the author's house wrote to express his regret that he had not made fuller use of his opportunities for beating him and his hope that others would make good the deficiency.[9] *The Times* reviewer was particularly outraged by a scene depicting two Eton masters in a nightclub accompanied by ladies of easy virtue. Toadying and philistinism are perhaps the most prominent targets of a somewhat indiscriminate attack but snobbery is well to the fore.

The three authors more nearly contemporary with Henry Green and more nearly his equals in reputation, George Orwell, Cyril Connolly and Anthony Powell, provide matter for debate. On the evidence of *A Question of Upbringing* one would not have thought that Eton, incurious, self-satisfied and eccentric though it might appear, was snobbish. It was not a world that looked down on others so much as a world that did not look. But unlike the author of *Decent Fellows* Anthony Powell is an imaginative artist. His book was not written to praise or censure Eton. Connolly and Orwell on the other hand are men with a message, the one as a social critic the other as the historian of his own aesthetic development. Orwell's attitude to Eton is at first sight contemptuous if not hostile. 'Five years in a lukewarm bath of snobbery,' the characteristically pungent phrase in which he dismisses the subject matter of Connolly's much admired account of the Eton they knew, does not suggest

---

7 *Pack My Bag*, 136 – 7.
8 John Heygate, who shortly after ran off with Evelyn Waugh's first wife.
9 E.C.C. 2155/952, 956.

that he thought much of it. But the force and simplicity of Orwell's writing was not achieved without sometimes making his opinions or his recollections appear rather starker than they were. It seems, in fact, that he enjoyed Eton. He concedes as much at the conclusion of his justly famous and ferocious attack on his preparatory school, *Such, Such Were the Joys*.[10] 'I have never even been down to Eton, where I was relatively happy, though I did once pass through it in 1933 and noted with interest that nothing seemed to have changed, except that the shops now sold radios.' Perhaps less had changed even than Orwell thought, for William Johnson Cory had told the Royal Commission on the Public Schools that Eton boys wasted too much time, especially in looking in at shop-windows.[11] The argument from silence is often unconvincing but it is difficult to believe that the greatest pamphleteer since Hazlitt would have chosen an obscure private school for his target if Eton had exemplified the snobbery and toadying he wished to pillory.

Cyril Connolly made something very different out of their common experience. He was himself, as he disarmingly admits, a well-informed and conscious snob so that he was to an unusual degree aware of the refinements and potentialities of this engrossing hobby that Eton had to offer. These were not to be found in the crude pursuit of titled acquaintance but in the class structure special to the boy world. Here from the beginning the line of division lay between Colleger and Oppidan. It had for centuries been deep and wide but the evidence put before the Royal Commission in the sixties is unanimous that it had been much diminished by the reforms initiated by Provost Hodgson. Connolly's view links social snobbery to anti-intellectualism:

> It was not smart at Eton to work; to be a 'sap' was a disgrace
> and to compete for prizes eccentric ... Even in College,
> among the seventy scholars, 'sapping' was discredited, and
> we were infected by the fashion from without, behind which
> lay the English distrust of the intellect, and prejudice in

10 *Collected Essays* (Penguin ed. 1970), IV, 379 – 422.
11 *Etoniana* 74/383.

favour of the amateur. A child in Ireland, a boy at St Wul-
fric's [the prep school he and Orwell had attended], a scholar
at Eton, I had learnt the same lesson. To be 'highbrow' was
to be different, to be set apart, and excluded from the ruling
class ... Intelligence was a deformity which must be concealed ... As opposed to ability, it was a handicap in life.

At Eton this was emphasised by the stigma attaching to
Collegers, which although an economic prejudice, was expressed as an anti-intellectual one and of which a ridiculous
aspect was the contempt in which boys held masters, a relic
of the eighteenth century, when boys brought their own
tutors to Eton and treated them, as the term 'usher' still
indicated, little better than their servants. In this direction the
feeling was strong, masters who were old Etonians, who
were rich like John Christie, or well-born like Georgie
Lyttelton, escaped, but in general the boys assumed that most
of the staff had never held a gun, or worn a tailcoat, that they
were racked by snobbery, by the desire to be asked to stay
with important parents, or to be condescended to by popular
boys.[12]

Neither the grammar nor the history in the second paragraph
of this quotation shows the author at his best. Boys brought
tutors to Eton well before the eighteenth century and the term
'usher' goes back almost to the foundation. It was in fact
applied to the first master appointed to assist the single master
of the original charter. The two thus became known in course
of time as Head Master and Lower Master. The confusion
between 'tutor' and 'usher' is thus the one real mistake of substance it is possible to make in this limited topic.

But false analysis does not imply false observation. It was
certainly true that a stigma still attached to Collegers when I
went to the school twenty years later. More accurately perhaps
a potential stigma as one was only made aware of it by boys who
were no doubt conscious of their own inferior position in the
school and wanted to take it out on someone else. Still, the term
'tug', derived from 'togatus' the Latin for gowned, was meant
to be offensive, though often used good-humouredly, and there

12 *Enemies of Promise,* 275 – 6.

was no reciprocally insulting description of Oppidans. Was the derision that of the social snob or of the football hooligan? I think the second now but may have felt the first at the time. It was so much mixed up with the unfamiliarities and insecurities of one's first year that distinctness of recollection and objectivity of interpretation are difficult and probably untrustworthy. Documentary evidence bearing on this point is not easy to find. But Dr Alington preserved in his scrapbook part of a trials* answer, written about 1927, which he must have thought curious for precisely this reason:

> Another example of small things making great differences in everyday life is a boy who is known as a tug among all Oppidans, who by getting some desease does a wonderful service to the whole school, for because of the desease no boy may come into collision with a boy of any other school and therefore may not go to camp. The only remark made by Oppidans is 'Hurrah, no camp! first good turn a tug has done us for years.'[13]

As to Connolly's contention that the mere fact of working lowered a boy in social esteem, classed him as a player and not a gentleman in the terminology of a famous cricket fixture of the period, there is, and probably always will be, some truth in that. No doubt the term 'sap' is originally offensive and was often so used in my time. But we also used it in a purely neutral sense, 'sapping for an examination, sapping up tomorrow's construe'. There have always been philistines at Eton or anywhere else, and philistines are by nature domineering. But unless one was unlucky enough to be in a house where they had the bit between the teeth it was possible to take no notice of them. At an earlier period than Connolly's Maurice Baring, himself an Oppidan, records a school life of incessant and apparently undisturbed, even approved, literary study. 'I enjoyed Eton from the first moment I arrived.' When he was told by his uncle, Sir Henry Ponsonby, private secretary to Queen Victoria, that

---

* Trials is the name given to the examinations held at the end of each term ('half' in the Eton language).
13 Scrapbook (unfoliated) in the possession of his daughter Lady Home.

he had won the Prince Consort's French Prize (the Queen herself was the first to be informed) '... nothing in after life could ever touch the rapture of the moment when I knew I had got it'.[14]

More difficult to follow is the epigrammatic suggestion in Connolly's first paragraph: 'Intelligence was a deformity ... as opposed to ability it was a handicap in life.' In this passage Connolly is of course stating the values on which Eton life was based, not expressing his own opinions. Yet unless we know what distinction, in this context, he is drawing between intelligence and ability the meaning is far from clear. He earlier records his pleasure in being praised by one master whom he admired and by another whom he did not for being 'v. able.'[15] To interpret 'intelligence' as aesthetic or literary perception as distinct from mental or intellectual capacity (which the system approved) does not help matters because the whole argument is derived from the 'anti-intellectual prejudice' of the place. Something no doubt is being said but it is hard to say what.

What of Connolly's account of the view taken of the masters by the boys? How accurate a representation is it and what substance, if any, underlay it? Evidence could be adduced for and against: of Connolly's own contemporaries already cited Lord Home would be against and Henry Green would be for. To assume a superiority over people set in authority over oneself gratifies self-esteem. To advertise it solicits admiration. That there will always be boys, and not only boys, to draw attention to themselves in this way seems obvious. But was it really the majority view? Not, certainly, in my time twenty years after Connolly, when beaks were judged largely by whether they kept us interested or amused. If they satisfied that criterion, almost any degree of good relations from liking to close friendship might follow, depending on how much one had to do with them. If they failed then indeed all their personal qualities, appearance, intelligence, habits, social origins, offered material

14 *The Puppet Show of Memory* (1922), 87, 116.
15 *op. cit.* 256.

for disparagement. Otherwise we were not interested in their antecedents. One generally knew whether they had themselves been to Eton, not out of any curiosity but probably out of subconscious recognition of trivialities. I do not remember that anyone thought the more or the less of them on that account. Some of the teaching was unquestionably brilliant but like so much else at Eton its strength lay in the virtuoso performance rather than in the general level. On the classical side there were first-rate scholars who made learning a pleasure without disguising its rigours, Francis Cruso and Denys Wilkinson prominent among them. Of the history masters of my time none reached the heights of Henry Marten though J.D. Hills had the real teacher's knack of interesting the dull as well as the imaginative. Perhaps the outstanding class-room teacher was William Hope-Jones, a mathematician of some distinction. In the tradition of Cory he paid little attention to the syllabus, but took immense trouble to make the content of his subject real to his auditors. To bring home the geometrical concept known as π which schoolboys encounter when they are taught how to calculate the area of a circle he used to bring into school a large round cake, cooked by his wife, which was then cut into slices and rearranged in the form of a rectangle. His eccentricities were of a kind usually associated with a self-consciously progressive school. He was a fanatic for physical fitness, and a passionate advocate of eugenics and of nudism. Practising the second of these beliefs on a beach in Wales where he erroneously thought himself unobserved brought him into the police court and the newspapers.

Were some of the masters snobs and social climbers? Perhaps one or two: and certainly two of the wives were notorious for their tireless pursuit of titled parents. What was much more in evidence was the traditional internal snobbery of the public school, the desire of the housemaster to fill his list not with earls or marquises but with members of the Eleven or the Eight, to count among his boys the Keeper of the Field or the Keepers of Fives. There were two house-masters in my time who were bywords for their success in this strenuous competition and two or three more who laboured in their wake. The type, timeless in character however he may change in superficialities, is caught once and for all by G.F. Bradby in *The Lanchester Tradition*. What adds piquancy at Eton to the housemaster's gratification at winning House Cups or having the Captain of the Eleven under his roof is the probability, the near-certainty, that he will have more members of Pop in his house than any of his rivals.

Childish though this may seem, Pop, or the Eton Society to give it its official title, was the real focus of snobbery at Eton between the wars. In its origins a political debating society strictly forbidden to frame any motion that might have the remotest contemporary relevance it had retained its right to elect its own members and had acquired formidable powers over other Etonians. When Mr Gladstone who had made his first speech as a member of that body revisited Eton in the seventies he enquired 'whether any athletes were admitted into "Pop" adding that in his day they liked to have the Captain of the Boats in the Society if possible, to show that they had no prejudice against athletics.'[16] The question was received with polite amusement since by then the society was largely composed of the best games players. Nonetheless there have always been some members elected for other reasons: because they were widely liked and respected, because they were close friends of senior and influential members or, sometimes, because they were very good company or of such intellectual distinction that they impressed even an electorate of such lilies of the field. Thus in the period just before the First World War an outstandingly brilliant generation of Collegers was represented by, among others, Ronald Knox and Patrick Shaw-Stewart. When Shaw-Stewart was killed in action at the end of 1917 his obituarist (probably Alington, newly appointed Head Master, who as Master in College had known and loved him as a boy) wrote: 'It may be doubted whether there has ever been a boy at Eton whose intellect was from the first so mature, or who had so clear

16 A.C. Benson *Fasti Etonenses*, 494.

and rapid an insight into an argument.'[17] Yet even so powerful
a mind could be agitated by the approach of an election to Pop:

> I freely confess that the pondering of this question occupied
> me in the period between bed and sleep, and that I went so
> far as to make up lists of the electors and the dangers from
> black balls potentially wielded by each. There is certainly a
> vital anxiety surrounding the entrance to Pop – an anxiety to
> which the proudest cannot be indifferent, an entrance which
> the most assured cannot take for granted. To judge by the
> amount of open courtship which takes place, the volume of
> self-questioning such as mine must be proportionately vast.
> Probably I was one of those accused of courtship. Certainly
> as the half went on I emerged, to my own astonishment, from
> tuggish seclusion, and was admitted to the smiles and nods
> of the main body of Pop, and to the intimacy of its intellectual
> clique.[18]

Cyril Connolly's account of his manœuvres outruns anything
that could be recognized as courtship. No doubt he wishes to
shock as well as to amuse his readers:

'At that time Pop were the rulers of Eton, fawned on by
masters, and the helpless Sixth Form. Such was their prestige
that some boys who failed to get in never recovered; one was
rumoured to have procured his sister for the influential members.'

This course was not open to Connolly, an only child. But he
did what he could:

'I now admitted to myself my ambition to get into Pop, and
planned my campaign. My handicap was that I had no colour,
nor was I in Sixth Form, from which a certain number of Pops
had to be chosen. I could only hope to be elected as a wit.
Although it was but a small section of Pop who thought me
funny, they were influential.'[19]

He goes on to explain in detail the tactics that brought success. He took care to be seen walking arm-in-arm, a privilege

17 E.C.C. (1918), 366 – 7.
18 Ronald Knox *Patrick Shaw-Stewart*, 20 – 21.
19 *op. cit.* 299 ff.

restricted to Pop, with such members as he already knew well and talking to those with whom his acquaintance was slighter. The glamour of Pop was enhanced by the extraordinary and arbitrary powers conferred by membership. They could beat anyone and fag any lower-boy, powers otherwise strictly confined to the particular house in which one happened to be. In Connolly's time one could even be beaten for not knowing a member of Pop by sight. If this customary right survived into my day I do not remember hearing of its exercise. But with him, as with most others who yearned to be elected, it was not the substance but the externals of élitism that he craved. Beating and fagging disgusted him. Snobbery not lust for power was the spur.

It could, then, be argued that Eton made and accepted payments in snobbery even if the currency was of purely local value. Life there taught those who were willing to learn the lessons of social climbing, but it also taught one to despise them. 'I mention this,' says Connolly of the arts he employed to attain membership of Pop, 'in case it may be of use to others who wish to be elected to things.'[20] By no means all the members of Pop found it necessary or would have found it tolerable to compass their election by such means. Most of them were, so to speak, inevitable members through their success at games. The climate of Eton opinion in the twenties and thirties, admirably rendered in Anthony Powell's series of novels already mentioned was detached and sceptical. Widmerpool, its most famous creation, was not, it will be remembered, ever taken so seriously by those who had been his contemporaries there as by the world in general. We do not know what Connolly's schoolfellows thought of his machinations but it would be very surprising if under such critical eyes they passed unobserved.

The more distant the view of Eton College the more prominent appears its concern with titles and ancient families. Close to, one is not, or was not when I was there from 1938 to 1942, aware of it. When I went there I do not think I had met a peer and I was certainly ignorant of elementary principles that

20 *ibid.*

regulate courtesy titles, prefixes and the rest. Finding onself next to a boy with a title one perceived as Pepys did on getting to know Charles II 'that the King is a man like other men'. Perhaps some boys touched with romanticism or tinged with snobbery sought the company of those so distinguished. But there was no general interest in the matter, certainly no tacit deference as there was to the best games players. Outside it was very different. Everyone who disapproved of Eton was sure that it taught us all to suck up to the aristocrats. Those who had no connexion with the place but wished to establish one were apt to believe that social prominence qualified them to do so. It is well known that Hitler's close associate Ribentrop when German ambassador in London requested a place for his son at short notice. Claude Elliott, then Head Master, politely but firmly protested his inability to arrange this.[21] That this mistaken assumption was not confined to foreigners is clear from the following letter, written by a ruffled peer, preserved by its recipient, Cyril Alington, in his scrapbook.

8 March 1920

Sir,

I am in receipt of your letter of the 5th inst. in which you state that you do not think that there will be a vacancy for my son in 1926 but if I cared to satisfy myself then I could write to about a dozen different housemasters.

This I have no intention of doing. For one of my name and position you should have made a vacancy.[22]

A better-tempered example may be drawn from personal recollection. My father, a country clergyman, and my mother were being entertained in the early thirties by a local landowner of long and impeccable ancestry. The hostess politely asked my mother where her children were at school. On being informed that my eldest brother was in his last year at Eton she paused in evident perplexity.

'Eton?' she said. 'Not ... not *our* Eton?'

---

21 Personal information from the Head Master. I asked him about it when a boy at the school late in 1940.
22 Holograph MS *loc. cit.*

CHAPTER TEN

Lengthening Shadows

BETWEEN THE TWO WORLD WARS Eton had two Provosts, M.R. James and Lord Hugh Cecil (subsequently created Lord Quickswood by his old friend Winston Churchill) and two Head Masters, Cyril Alington and Claude Elliott. In those decades the number of boys in the school was between 1100 and 1150. The number of masters was generally round eighty or ninety. Thus in round figures about five thousand boys passed through the school in this period and something over a hundred masters taught there. A few of the masters were brief visitants. Every appointment was in the first instance probationary. Most came fresh from the university and were trying their wings. Thus the number of masters who had the opportunity of making themselves felt in the place was comparatively small. A great deal of this book has been devoted to showing how Eton had come to be what it was at various points in its history. It was, and is, a living institution, renewing itself as the human body renews itself until death cuts off the current, yet retaining all the time a discernible identity. Continuity has much to offer and much to impose. Structure, the concept that Braudel has made fundamental to history, sets limits to what is possible at any given moment. But the tone of an institution is that of the people who compose it. Evidently they themselves are to a degree shaped and influenced by the environment of ideas and traditions in which they live and work. Nonetheless the process is reciprocal.

Who were the dominant personalities, what were the leading ideas, what was the quality of life at Eton in this the closing period of the long classical and Christian ascendancy? A school that had suffered as Eton had in the First War must be conscious of its ghosts. And ghosts perhaps enhance the veneration habitually accorded to the very old. There were still, when the war ended, distinguished ex-masters living at Eton, Ainger and Luxmoore, who had been colleagues of William Johnson Cory. Luxmoore died in 1926, the year in which a young Balliol man, Robert Birley, who was staying on to read Modern Greats after getting his First in history accepted an invitation to teach at Eton. Luxmoore's influence made itself felt not only directly through his patriarchal appearance and his disciplined and powerful personality but indirectly through the deep admiration and affection in which the Provost held him. And has any figure in the whole history of Eton, master, Head Master, Provost or Vice-Provost, with the possible but shadowy exception of John Hales, been held in such universal esteem as Provost James? What these men were and stood for has been sufficiently indicated. How profound were the feelings of M.R. James, a naturally reserved man, for his old tutor may be judged from the address he delivered to the school at Evensong on the first Sunday after his death. He touched lightly but tellingly on his benefactions to the school and on the even greater benefits he had conferred by preserving its most beautiful buildings from destruction and quoted his own watchword:

'To us the ages have bequeathed somewhat of which we are but guardians for our time: the continuity of Eton history and much of the best power of her influence are lost if we abuse that trust.'

He stressed the severity, even the rigour, of his standards.

'Faithfulness was the mark of him everywhere: in religion, in duty, in criticism, above all in friendship.' And he placed the full weight of this tribute from the heart on Luxmoore's religion.

'Nobody ever loved Eton more truly and faithfully than my tutor; and this Chapel was the centre and pivot of his love; for he knew that all the things that are best about Eton come from God, and he took every opportunity of thanking God for them here and praying to Him that they might continue and be increased. And I do not doubt that he so thanks God and prays to Him for Eton still.'[1]

This was no ordinary recitation in reverently appreciative tones of the achievements and qualities fit to be recorded on such an occasion but a confession of faith. One cannot imagine an eighteenth century Provost, Bland or Sleech for instance, saying anything of the kind. Nor, come to that, Henry Marten or Claude Elliott, both of whom in time were to succeed James in the Provostship. Both men were punctilious in discharging their responsibilities, the one as Vice-Provost and the other as Head Master, in attendance at chapel: but it was rather as if they were walking in the Lord Mayor's procession. Alington's religious influence and in particular his gifts as a preacher have already been mentioned. Yet the tide of opinion and habit in the early twenties was running strongly against religious belief and observance. Regular attendance at public worship had plummeted. In intellectual circles Christianity was likely to be regarded as a fad. Inevitably such tendencies made themselves felt at Eton. A sceptical worldliness is congenial to its easy-going style. And the young Collegers were ready and anxious to rid themselves of any inherited intellectual baggage that could be left behind with a good conscience. Lord Hailsham, who was regarded by his contemporaries in College as the leader of reaction against the liberalism of the Orwell-Connolly era, records a schoolboy encounter with Alington, who had come to console him on the sudden death of his mother. 'He was a gentleman and a Christian. He sought to console me with talk about the after life. I was discourteous. I suddenly realized that I did not believe a word of what he was saying, and I told him so. I said that I believed that when we died we were nothing. "Like the animals," I said, for good measure. He was angry and went away.'[2] The distress of the circumstances makes this easy to understand. But in general Alington showed tolerance and wisdom in his handling of boys who professed unbelief, as,

1 reprinted in E.C.C. 6/12/26.
2 *The Door Wherein I Went* (1975), 7.

for instance, in the case of Orwell himself.[3] His boldness was his strength in defending what he believed in. Not only did the classics thrive under him but he came near to substituting Greek for Latin as the main language in the teaching of the subject.[4] This would have been a dashing manoeuvre at any time; the more then when the classical supremacy was challenged.

His appointments to the staff showed flair and freshness. An Oxford man himself he chose outstanding Cambridge scholars to uphold the standard of the classics. A Conservative in politics (at General Elections he did not cast his vote, preferring to make a permanent pair with his wife who would have voted Labour) he recruited a number of radical young men including a science master whose wife made no secret of her membership of the Communist Party. Like his brother-in-law Edward Lyttelton he invited an ex-chairman of the T.U.C to address the school, or rather the senior part of it known as the First Hundred, in 1920.[5] In 1921 no invitations were issued to the usual Fourth of June festivities and there were no fireworks 'in consequence of the national crisis' (perhaps a dignified description of a railway strike which might, in that less motorised age, have made attendance difficult).[6] A fortnight earlier the *Eton College Chronicle* had carried the obituary of a man who had attended the last Montem celebrations as a boy of 12. So strong are the echoes in such a place. Sometimes they are mercifully distant as when in 1924 General Sir George Higginson, at 98 the oldest surviving Old Etonian general, took the salute at the march past of the Company Cup and addressed the two winning companies on his early experiences in the Crimea.[7]

Alington's direction was imaginative and stimulating and, in particular, responsive to the world around him. But A.C. Benson who, it will be remembered, championed his appointment was surely shrewd in his judgment that the Head Master was

---

3 Stansky & Abrahams *The Unknown Orwell*.
4 C.A. Alington *Things Ancient and Modern*.
5 E.C.C. 19/11/20.
6 *ibid* 19/5/21.
7 *ibid* 26/6/24.

'very conventional in his ambitions'. Was it necessary to bring back the birch? Would it not have been better to discourage if not to prohibit the very free use of the cane permitted to adolescents? Did so old and self-confident an institution have to fuss about minute particularities of protocol, with a high seriousness reminiscent of Carlyle making fun of the *ancien régime*? The prohibition on having one's head uncovered – a top hat if in school dress, a cap if changed for games – on walking on the east side of Eton High Street, on turning down the collar of one's greatcoat, all these taboos could be and often were enforced by beating. When other schools were wisely harnessing the strong and often enriching urge to act, the drama was discouraged at Eton until at last permission for the performance of a school play was granted in 1931. Even then it had for some years to be the play chosen by the School Certificate examiners as a set book. The same year witnessed the founding of a Film Society.[8] For a school with the tradition of speeches behind it, to say nothing of the Shakespeare Society, this was carrying conservatism far. Speeches, the delivery on the Fourth of June of a declamation from history or literature in its original language by each member of Sixth Form, persisted in its traditional form and in the traditional dress such as must have been worn by the young Lord Wellesley when he moved George III to tears by his rendering of Strafford's great defence to his impeachment.

What overwhelms all criticism of Alington's régime is its openness of heart and mind. How much of this might come from the love of her neighbour that Mrs Alington's life so fully expressed, how much from the extraordinary kindness and accessibility of the Provost need not be assessed. The three are merged in the recollection of the boys and masters who knew Eton in their time and it seems unnecessary to disentangle a fabric so closely woven. In this they upheld the great tradition, admired by Benson in his encomium of Cory, that consciously set the affections above the intellect. The point of that tradition is that it does not abate the claims that education must make for

8 For much of this information I am indebted to Mr P.S.H. Lawrence.

mental excellence. It simply says that however high they are put, the claims of the individual must be put higher. This is the root idea, manifested in the room of one's own and in the tutorial system, so akin to that of the university, to which the formal teaching of the classroom is secondary. Its essence is personal, its habits informal: and it will work only where there is a degree of intimacy. Alington records how shocked and horrified Warden Anson of All Souls was at his description of the easy relations between masters and boys that he found at Eton at the turn of the century. He himself became at once, and as Head Master steadfastly remained, its champion. 'The pupil-room system' he wrote in retirement, 'provides for a closeness of . . . intercourse and a permanency of relationship between boy and master which does not, so far as I know, exist elsewhere. Eton may, or may not, be "the best of schools" but there is no school where it is so easy for a boy and a master to know one another well. What is elsewhere the fortunate possession of a few is at Eton the inheritance of all.'[9]

Perhaps a word should be said here about those terms, ubiquitous in Eton life, 'tutor' and 'pupil-room'. Tutors, in the ordinary sense, had first been employed at Eton in the eighteenth century by rich parents concerned to remedy the deficiencies of the enormous classes. Gradually the school incorporated the function as more and more of the masters supplemented their salaries by undertaking private tuition for a fee. The pupils of any particular master were collectively said to be 'in his pupil-room' as opposed to being 'up to him', which would mean that they were in his division for the regular work of the school. The distinction is made even clearer by the term 'Private Business' (see p. 186). Since classics was, until the later nineteenth century, the only subject officially taught, the tutor was, inevitably, a classical master. Even in the twenties and thirties every boy on entering the school was assigned to a classical tutor who would be responsible for his general intellectual culture and academic progress. Were the housemaster himself a classic he usually took the boy into his own pupil-room. If, after taking

9 *Things Ancient and Modern*, 98.

present Emperor of Japan when Crown Prince in May 1921. 'H. Babington Smith K.S., Acting Captain of the School, standing in front of the statue, pronounced clearly and effectively a form of welcome in Japanese, to which the school responded with a shout of "Banzai"...'[2]

Boys from other houses were encountered in the classroom, at Private Business with one's tutor, in the Corps, on the cricket field (if one was a dry bob), in the host of voluntary societies or if one played some optional game such as Rugby or Association football or went beagling. In practice this generally meant that, outside his own house, a boy might have an acquaintance, mostly of the slightest, of forty or fifty of his contemporaries. To have known half a dozen well would have been an achievement unless athletic eminence had hoisted him to a wider view. Similarly unless he was a member of Pop there was no place of common resort where people from different houses could meet without previous arrangement. The social rewards of success at games were therefore huge. If one wanted to be well known or to command a wide circle of friends this was virtually the only means of scaling the walls of the house system.

College was, from this point of view, better off, since it was about twice the size of an Oppidan house. And it would have been very surprising if the fact of being elected by competitive examination had not produced a certain activity of mind, a readiness to talk and argue and read and enquire, that in itself engendered friendships. How cultivated and how enduring these could be can be seen from Noel Blakiston's publication of the letters written to him by Connolly. The correspondence did not long survive matrimony. 'It is impossible I think to continue to exact from life the standards one has acquired from literature single-handed' wrote Connolly in 1929. 'The world as opposed to Eton and Cambridge has such an undertow towards obscurity, blankness and Scotland standing where it did, that without a better half one is bound to succumb – and most people do when they've got one.'[3] Yet any society as individualist

2 E.C.C.
3 *A Romantic Friendship*: The letters of Cyril Connolly to Noel Blakiston (1975), 324.

as Eton must risk exposing its members to loneliness. 'If I was in the main not happy there ...' writes Professor Ayer 'it was because I got on badly with the other boys in College. This was very largely my own fault. I was too pleased with my own cleverness and I had a sarcastic tongue ... I wanted to be liked but did not know how to set about it.'[4] Such experience was commoner in an Oppidan house where the range of companion-ship available was anyhow more restricted.

The sense of Eton's largeness, almost to the extent of its being impersonal, was borne in on one in a number of ways. The use of printing where any other school would have used a typewritten or manuscript cyclostyled sheet was one. The weekly orders of the Corps, the timetable for each classical division (perhaps consisting of some thirty boys), the week's services in chapel, all were printed, as were the lists of member-ship of the school societies. One's clothes vanished and reap-peared by previous arrangement with one of the tailors in the High Street. Only school dress and the approved rig of the day for games might be kept in one's room. Top hats which were only discarded after the outbreak of war needed the periodic attentions of an expert. The rough treatment to which they were constantly exposed dishevelled their black silk strands. Smoothing with the hand could not make the transition from horrescence to sleekness. A craftsman with a brush and a hot iron, himself wearing the light white cotton cap immortalized by Tenniel's drawings of the Carpenter in *Through the Looking Glass*, was in constant, silent, attendance at the back of New and Lingwood's shop. Our hats joined the queue on the sloping board inside his sanctum (itself recorded in a painting hung in the Royal Academy in 1926) while we awaited their return to civilization in an anteroom supplied with copies of the *Sphere* and the *Sketch*, handsomely produced illustrated magazines that did not discolour the reader's hands with unwholesome smell-ing ink. There was an air of remoteness about the proceeding that was in a way refreshing because in any community the pressure of other people's personalities becomes, like the noise

4 A. J. Ayer, *op.cit.* 57.

level of a city, a background whose sudden obliteration is always grateful. But it did also suggest that Eton was a metropolis rather than a village.

For the masters and their wives the reverse was true. There were, naturally, far fewer of them and the hospitality of the place, providing constant and agreeable opportunities for gossip, meant that everyone knew everyone else and everything that was to be known about them. Social life revolved round the dinner party. Cocktails and sherry parties which had established themselves pretty generally in England by the middle twenties did not fit in to the Eton *train de vie*. In the winter halves masters would be taking private business, in the summer out on the playing fields or the river, until bare time was left to change into a dinner-jacket and arrive at their host's. The timing of an Eton dinner-party prescribed its pattern. When dessert was reached, shortly before nine, the housemasters present returned to their houses to conduct prayers and thereafter to make the circuit of the house. At ten o'clock, the time for lights out, they would re-join the party they had left. As in the style of life at Oxford or Cambridge the presence of servants to cook and clear away, to lay the fires and clean the rooms, was assumed. In the twenties and thirties it was not a large assumption. Not until the Second World War did the number of people working in factories approach the figure of those engaged in domestic service.

In the early part of the period it would not have been hard to imagine Eton, shops and all, as a loose-jointed Collegiate society. There was next to no traffic. At midnight the master and his wife who lived at the River House could walk home from a dinner-party along the crown of the road to Windsor Bridge, fearing no onrush of headlights and hearing nothing but the laughter and talk of other masters parting on the doorsteps of their lodgings further down the High Street. After the trenches from which so many of the younger men had survived such a society, self-sufficient but various, rooted but pushing out new shoots, naturally attracted a loyalty and an affection of exclusive intensity. Perhaps there was loss as well as gain in this. Much of what men such as Cory and Benson had to contribute came from their dissatisfaction with what Eton was and did. Great institutions are proportionately more prone to self-love and self-flattery. The larger the society the easier for men of intelligence to become absorbed in its life. Eton was large. There were always cultivated and amusing people among those who taught there. The charms of its society must have made it easy for it to be pre-occupied with itself.

Not that the Eton masters of the twenties and thirties did not include the dull and the boorish, the pretentious and the dim. Some with admirable qualifications for one part of the job lacked the combination required for the whole. J.F Crace who was Master in College in the time of Connolly and Orwell was much liked by his colleagues and admired as a scholar but he had none of Alington's flair for handling high-mettled young intellectuals. H.K. Marsden who succeeded him has received a report as cutting as any of his own from Professor Ayer.[5] Marsden, he points out, was obsessed by his connexion with the school which lasted from the day he was elected to a scholarship to his reluctant acceptance of retirement, excepting only the absences necessary to secure a university degree and that imposed by war service, which he spent in regulating railway timetables. In the universal havoc and dislocation here at least was a 'single talent well employ'd'. Regulations, and the penalties attendant on their infringement, were his ruling passion. It is ironic indeed that a spirit so essentially hostile to everything that Eton stood for should have cast himself for the role of guardian of its traditions. His siege mentality evoked loyalty and *esprit de corps* from the boys in his house, whom he defended, like some clan chieftain, from the official punishments he was zealous in securing for everyone else. If his boys were to be chastised he desired to be the sole arbiter and, it was said, executor of the matter. Deplorable as all this might be it seems to have worked. His house was a good one by the only known tests, namely that his boys seemed generally happy and successful

---

5 *op.cit.* 48–9. Crace is the [unnamed] Master in College in *Enemies of Promise*. See also on him Stansky and Abrahams *The Unknown Orwell*, a much more reliable work, for this period at least, than Prof. Crick's biography.

and their subsequent contribution to the life of the nation has not been negligible. The founder of the Landmark Trust and the inventor of radio-carbon dating have both come from that stable.

Marsden's next-door neighbour in the Eton Wick Road illustrates the contrasts of the place. A kindly, sentimental enthusiast who would never have thought of punishing anyone for anything, he lived for fox-hunting and high churchmanship. There was even a small shrine in the dusty, chalk-smelling division room in which, with an emotion and an effervescence not usually associated with the subject, he taught us mathematics. On his retirement he hunted for a season with the Fernie and then became a monk. His house, despite his own transparent goodness, had a bad reputation. Perhaps each of the two concerned himself to a degree that seemed excessive with elements of Eton life that were generally accepted without comment, in the one case religion and in the other school rules. But the convention that enforcement of disciplinary regulations was left to the senior boys made it almost a breach of manners for a master to occupy himself with the matter. Religion was at once a more delicate issue and a less clearly defined territory. The school as a religious foundation, the housemaster in the course of his general responsibilities, the tutor in his nominally more intellectual ones, all had theoretically or practically an interest in this most personal and yet most public question.

Most public because it occasioned the only daily gathering of the school as a whole, or rather in two unequal portions, as the Lower Boys attended Lower Chapel while all the rest of the school, Jews and Roman Catholics excepted, filled College Chapel. 'Filled' is no exaggeration. 'Crammed' would convey more exactly the impression one had as a service was about to begin. It was reinforced by the singing of the hymns and the psalms. Henry Ley, the organist, understood and enjoyed the potentialities of seven hundred male voices. There was a simplicity and a grandeur that most found moving and nearly all found memorable. Everyone knows that a crowded theatre, a crowded House of Commons, elicits a performance or heightens an atmosphere in an extraordinary way. The jostling congregation of College Chapel offered the same opportunity which Alington, brilliantly, took.

It also offered the opportunity for nimble misbehaviour of the kind that schoolboys especially appreciate. The Conduct, as the chaplain who took the service was called (for the same reason as a *condottiere*, namely that they were both hirelings) was a parson whose ultra-parsonical appearance and diction would have been thought excessive on the comic stage. As he drifted up the central aisle, his eyes lifted unseeingly to higher things, his surplice almost touching the black tail-coats of the boys standing in their places on either side, it was possible for the insolent and irreverent to wish him Good Morning without his being able to check his forward movement or to turn his head and take a name. A mild and minimal risk that one might be spotted by an unusually vigilant 'master-in-desk' lent an added spice. This trivial, the harsh would say pointless, detail would not be worth recording if it did not seem to sum up the Etonian public opinion of my day towards the official religion of the school. Partly it was the age-old schoolboy teasing of authority. Partly it was derisive of parsons, socially as a profession and theologically as possible pretenders to priestly functions that Broad Church Protestantism emphatically rejected. Lastly it was a gesture that could only be made if one was in chapel to make it.

The contradictions of the Eton religious tradition that we inherited matched those of the nation at large. After the strictness of the medieval foundation, the conformity of the Elizabethan period, the learned piety of the seventeenth century came the neglect and loutishness of the eighteenth which survived, somewhat modified by Keate's Draconian régime, into the time of Mr Gladstone. Gladstone's own profound sense of religion and his urgent High Churchmanship were anything but Etonian, and owed nothing to its traditions. 'Religion was nonexistent then at Eton' he told A.C. Benson who was his guest at Hawarden in 1897. 'I told my father that I did not wish to be confirmed at Eton, but the fiat went out that I was to be included among the candidates. The order was given us all for a book of sermons – but we never got it, though our parents paid for it, and Pote [the Eton bookseller] had the money. We were never asked if we read it – I went three times to Knapp, my tutor. He came out of his study – took up a volume of Sinclair's sermons – there was not an ounce of Christianity in them – read a couple of pages, shut the book up with a snap – said "you can go" and walked out. Three times this happened, and never another word of advice.'

'The administration of the Sacrament was a scandal. The etiquette in the school was that no one should receive except the Sixth Form, and they were obliged to. I don't suppose there was ever an official pronouncement on this – but the authorities must have noticed it, and they never contradicted the idea.'[6] Gladstone's own conspicuous reverence when revisiting Eton Chapel was admired if it was not imitated. But even he, in anything to do with religion the least characteristic of Etonians, could not altogether escape its influence. Talking to Benson of Keate's reading Blair's sermons to the school and then giving out notices he remembered '... the boys booing Keate – a humming noise with lips closed (he illustrated this by booing loudly) – so that Keate could never detect the offenders; "a truly British national thing that – I fear it has died out?" "Yes," I said. "I am sorry," he replied, "that booing has died out – it gives us a sense of our national privilege of disagreeing with constituted authority." '[7]

The elements of the past were contained in the formalities and the tone of the twenties and thirties. The boy who avowed himself agnostic was uncommon but the weight of outside opinion, certainly of fashionable opinion, bore against religious belief. Missions and voluntary services during Lent elicited an often surprisingly large response. This was of course no necessary indication of what people actually believed but was certainly evidence of a readiness to listen. No doubt a great deal depended on the particular circle of which each boy was a member, and that was, as has been said, a matter determined more by

6 A.C. Benson *Fasti Etonenses* (1899), 499. Mr. Gladstone's account of the restriction of the sacrament to the Sixth Form is confirmed, with every sign of approval, by Winthrop Mackworth Praed in a letter to his sister dated 5 Dec. 1819 printed in *Etoniana* 94/690.
7 *ibid.*

circumstance than choice. Here the personality and example of the housemaster could be of crucial importance. What was said, or left unsaid, when he went round the house every night seeing his boys on their own mattered much more than the jealously guarded right to prepare them for confirmation. In this context Jack Upcott comes at once to mind, a man of decided tastes (he forbade the use of the word 'picturesque' on the grounds that it was meaningless) and strong, if unaggressive, Christianity. As to the teaching, formal and informal, some of the masters whom I was up to let it be perceived that they were not committed to instructing us in Christian orthodoxy. A questioning irony was often applied to the hymns we had sung or even to the passage of scripture which the Provost had briefly expounded to us. We were not encouraged to sneer but we were encouraged to examine what a text said and to think what it meant. This indeed was the basis of the classical training then still in the ascendant. As I write I am thinking of Richard Martineau who for many years shared the teaching of the Head Master's Division, as the top classical set was traditionally called. He taught us to read the ancient authors as Cory prescribed – 'The Greeks expect you to be on your mettle when you read their books.' – and set us an example of swift and felicitous translation in which mind, imagination and sensibility were stretched to their full reach. And for classical specialists at least the matter of the ancient authors, their tone, their assumptions, were often so obviously and so self-confidently irreconcilable with the Christianity that only those who were ready to let the will do the work of the intellect could believe that its truths, if truths they were, were both easy and self-evident. Scholarship of any kind must inculcate a sceptical, critical habit of mind. Classical scholarship reinforces this by immersing the student in a literature of great power and beauty springing from an environment wholly different from his own. The antitheses of human experience, love and death, youth and age, of emotion, of morality stand out the more sharply because they are stripped of familiar accretions. A classical training teaches through the sensibilities what history can only impress on a developed mind, that people once saw things very differently from ourselves. To be provincial is surely to believe that anyone who does not think and act as we do is somehow odd and needs to explain himself. To recognise the possibility that one's own ideas and standards may require some explanation is the mark of a civilized and cultivated mind.

It would be manifestly absurd, besides being presumptuous, to claim that Etonians are never provincial or boorish. Too many examples to the contrary will come to mind to make any such assertion thinkable. But what may be fairly claimed for the classical teaching at Eton from Cory's time to the Second World War is that it offered abundantly the means of emancipation from provincialism and from received opinions: and that not the least of its virtues was that it left so much to the choice of the individual, even the deciding whether to make use of it or not. 'Sir, I have provided you with an argument: I am not obliged to provide you with an understanding.' So, rather rudely as some have thought, Dr Johnson expressed what with a silent civility Eton left to be inferred. This had been true even in the rough and brutal days of Keate, as Mr Gladstone testified in a letter he wrote to A.C. Benson a day or two after the dinner already mentioned.

Hawarden
August 26, 97

Dear Mr Benson,

When you gave me the pleasure of your company on Tuesday and indicated an intention of writing on the Keatian period, you made me very talkative, but there were two things I omitted to state.

1. One was that the Eton Masters of my day, to whatever criticisms they might be open, had a great deal to do, and may I think justly be considered hard workers.

2. The other was that while the teaching may be considered as narrow and as affording no proper aids to the pupil, in one point it was admirable, I mean its rigid, inflexible, and relentless accuracy. This property I think invaluable and indispensable. It has been my habit to say that at Eton in my day a boy might if he chose learn something, or might if he chose learn nothing, but that one thing he could not do, and that was to learn anything inaccurately.[8]

8 *ibid*, 505.

The quality that Mr Gladstone was here emphasizing is inherent in the classical training. It has been attacked and defended most often on this very point. Its opponents denounce it for constricting the developing mind and the free-ranging imagination in a straitjacket of grammatical pedantry. The very words that Mr Gladstone uses to praise they use to condemn. The rigidity is the rigidity of death, the inflexibility and relentlessness that of the parade-ground, if not of the prison. It is the old antithesis of discipline and freedom, for both of which Eton and England have been specially valued and admired. One has only to turn back a page or two to find Mr Gladstone championing the right of the boys to express their disapproval of the Head Master. This is the paradox on which an open, liberal society rests. It is easily represented by its enemies as muddle-headedness, self-contradiction, or, more harshly, cant.

To this may be added a further paradox, evident from Mr Gladstone's recollection and still true in the twenties and thirties, of the high pressure at which the masters worked and the idleness permitted to their pupils. In its highest view this was the freedom to choose, without which there can be no taste, and thus, according to Cory's standards, no truly Etonian education. This was certainly accepted by one of the liveliest and most delightful Eton masters of my time, Denys Wilkinson, who once observed to me that no system of education was worth anything if it did not give a boy the chance to be idle. To the stupid and the spoilt this did, no doubt, little good; to the vicious, possibly, harm. As the Provost gleefully reminded us there is no such thing as an equal opportunity. 'It's like saying that all button-holes must be equal, without taking account of the size of the buttons.' Even to the lazy and the listless, states of mind not uncommon in adolescence, it may have been a doubtful blessing. What gift, what privilege, is not open to large objections of possible abuse? Eton, endowed by the ages, was necessarily open to many.

CHAPTER THIRTEEN

Conclusion

IT WOULD BE POSSIBLE to fill several books with a rehearsal of the achievements and successes that could plausibly have been claimed for Eton in the twenties and the thirties. In politics and finance, in the diplomatic and administrative service of the government, in the army and the navy, at court and in the courts, the list of Old Etonians holding great positions should satisfy the proudest Old Boy. In other fields Maynard Keynes, J.B.S. Haldane and Aldous Huxley were at the height of their powers. Robert Bridges had been Poet Laureate and Gerald Kelly had been elected to the Royal Academy of which, soon after the Second War, he was to become President. In the priesthood Ronald Knox was Roman Catholic Chaplain to the University of Oxford while his brother Dillwyn had reluctantly surrendered a career as a classical scholar for a primacy in crypt-analysis that was to do the state some service. Sir Henry Segrave had broken the land speed record in his racing car and had lost his life in attempting to break the record on water. In county cricket, a sport that in the summers of the twenties and thirties dominated the public consciousness, Etonians were con-spicuous.

A further enumeration of triumphs and distinctions would be wearisome and irritating. It would also have little to do with the purpose of this book. It is obvious that many prominent figures in almost every part of the national life to which power or honour belong were Etonians. As a historical and sociological fact this is clearly of some importance. In France the system of the *grandes écoles*, to which entry is based on examinations, creates an élite of administrators, industrialists and financiers who share an experience and a culture that has been artificially contrived to fit them for eminence. They are, so to speak, the nation's racehorses. To what extent, if any, did this offer a parallel to Eton? In the most immediate sense that in both countries there was a circle of men with a much higher expectation of authority and influence than the general run of their compatriots, there was a likeness. And that was the feature that those outside at once recognized.

This fact in its turn affected the nature of the place. It was, by the twenties and thirties, well aware of its own importance – indeed had long been so. But a certain self-satisfaction, a feeling that the mere fact of being Etonian was in some way a cause for self-congratulation, may be detected. Rose, rosiest rose, became the dominant colour on the Etonian palette. Consider, for instance, the *Eton College Chronicle* reviewing Sir Shane Leslie's *The Oppidan* in March 1922: '. . . that he has genius his life of Cardinal Manning and many of his shorter poems exist to prove . . . Beautiful thoughts are scattered without effort in profusion through the book. "He loved the soft clay of boyhood, fresh from the mysterious and unaccountable Potter who planted the seed of such different flowers in such same-sized pots."' The critical reservation restricting the term 'genius' to some of Sir Shane's shorter poems is prudent. His epic poem on the battle of Jutland had won a reputation for absurdity that not even the piety of his old school could disguise.

Or take Hugh Macnaghten's *Fifty Years of Eton* published in 1924 in which superlatives cluster round everything Etonian from the view of Windsor Castle seen from the Brocas to the memorial inscriptions in the ante-chapel. The cult of Eton as a self-sufficient, self-renewing system offering an intellectual, moral, social and artistic explanation of life had established itself. In so doing it was false to the very things it purported to extol. Narcissism for all its seductive sentimentalities is nothing more than provincialism set to music. And it leads at once, as the examples cited too plainly show, to surrender of judgment and corruption of taste. 'Eton must continue to cultivate taste.' Cory's very success had its pitfalls. Macnaghten, as boy and master and Vice-Provost, had been deeply influenced by Lux-moore, was steeped in the same tradition as M.R. James.

For two centuries Eton had attracted the rich and the fashionable. From this quarter too the pressure of self-approval, enemy to all grace of mind and spirit, beat against the true genius of the place as Cory had perceived it. 'You go to a great school for self-knowledge.' You do not go to it for self-congratulation on the fact of having been there. Still less do you go to it in order to qualify for membership of some mafia or free-masonry that protects and prefers its own. Yet, in the general view, that is precisely what a number of people have sent their children to Eton for. It is the penalty of its standing. The tense is the historic present for it has long been so. The astute beneficiaries of a social system which Eton hall-marked and the romantic enthusiasts who find in the contemplation of the school a beatific vision to set against the vileness of the world have obscured the true value, the special quality, of the place.

And what, after so many hares have been started, was that? What principle underlay and reconciled the much-derided importance attached to the writing of Latin verses, the care lavished on the coaching of cricketers and oarsmen, the formality of dress, the informality of the greater part of the teaching? What drew men of high quality to the staff and held them there? If a single idea can be caught running through such diversity it is the idea of style. 'For God's sake, sir, if you must miss, do it in style.' Matt Wright's terse instruction recorded by Lord Home in his autobiography would surely have been approved by Cory. The classical education on which the curriculum was still based was, in its higher reaches, a training in style. It was not enough to understand what a Greek or Latin author was saying; one had to be able to explain how he said it. The style was to be attended to, as well as the content. In composition, that is the writing of Greek or Latin verse or prose, the engagement of meaning and style was even closer. The aim was to fuse the two. The point of the exercise was to enter into a mentality other than one's own, to imagine imitatively and to acquire the habit of intellectual detachment.

Style is in itself a liberal concept. It implies individuality and freedom of choice. And it implies plurality. The leisureliness, the comprehensiveness, the tolerance of the Eton régime of those days deriving from its aristocratic inheritance all favoured individual rather than corporate development. Its tradition of scholarship set a pattern of discipline. All this might, and often did, leave little impression on those to whom it was offered. But that was perfectly in character. The right to choose implies the right to reject.

That there were grave objections to the Eton I knew and whose nature I have tried to describe is a familiar fact. One would not have to read very far into the literature of the period to find them. On egalitarian grounds no defence can be constructed. To some that closes the question, to others not. Even to those who are ready to hedge their bets on equality, the extent of the freedom on which the system rested might seem an unjustifiable extravagance. Moving from social and economic generalities to intellectual and educational aims and methods, everyone knows the case against making the classics the foundation of the curriculum. That some of the most distinguished Eton masters were themselves well aware of it has been indicated earlier in this book.

To attempt to strike a balance on all these matters is to invite a rush of clichés to the head. I set out to try to catch a likeness of that multiple personality, a living institution that incorporates a long and continuous history, at a particular moment that seemed to me the culmination of a stage in its development. In any such attempt one is bound to make a host of judgments that reflect ideas, affections and prejudices that the reader may not share. The best one can do is to try to be aware that this is so. There is, after all, no consensus as to what society should be or what education is for. Until that point of unity is reached all judgment is more or less partial and the plurality for which Eton has stood may have its value in an unregenerate world.

GLOSSARY

Eton Expressions used in the text

Absence   A roll-call, usually held in School Yard. Presumably it took its name from the offence disclosed by failure to answer.

Chamber, Long Chamber   Up to the opening of the New Buildings in 1844 the seventy scholars lived and slept in the first-storey room that ran the length of the northern side of School Yard. After that date part of it accommodated the fifteen most junior Collegers in cubicles or 'stalls'.

Chambers   Usual abbreviation of 'Head Master's Chambers', the formal mid-morning meeting of all the masters. The Head Master's room was the rendez-vous.

College, Colleger   The scholars, collectively and individually, as opposed to Oppidan(s), see p. 19.

Conduct   Chaplain who took the service in College Chapel. So-called because he was hired, i.e. not a member of the Foundation.

Dame   A boarding-house keeper where a boy had lodgings. The term was used of men as well as women when they entered on this function, see p. 38.

Desk, In Desk   The vantage-point from which a master whose turn it was to maintain discipline in Chapel surveyed his charges.

Election   The totality of scholars elected in any one year. At any given moment College is composed of five elections.

Eton Society (Pop)   A self-co-opting club with important privileges and powers and an even more important mystique, see pp 147 − 8.

Half   What is elsewhere called a term. The word derives from the original division of the school year into two with only two short holidays.

Lower Master   Originally appointed to assist the Master (who, by the acquisition of this, his first, subordinate became 'Head Master') and long known as the Usher. As the school grew it became convenient to divide it into Upper and Lower. The Lower Master was thus assigned the educational and disciplinary responsibilities for the Lower Boys that the Head Master undertook for their seniors. The Lower Master in modern times is an ex-housemaster, appointed by the Head Master, whose place he takes in case of illness or absence.

Master-in-College   The housemaster in charge of the seventy scholars.

Oppidan   A boy who has not been elected to a scholarship, see p. 19.

Pop, see *Eton Society*.

Private Business   Tutorial as opposed to Classroom teaching, see p. 186.

Provost   The head of the Governing Body, see p. 28.

Pupil-Room   Collective term for the boys assigned to a particular tutor, see p. 156.

Sap   Verb, substantive and adjective indicating excessive intellectual activity.

Saying-Lesson   The learning by heart of a passage of verse, usually Latin or Greek, which one would be called on to repeat, beginning wherever the master chose. Thirty lines of Greek or Latin was the standard for the Head Master's Division.

Sixth Form   The ten senior Collegers and the ten senior Oppidans.

Trials   Examinations.

Tutor   see p. 156.

Up to   To be 'up to' a master is to be taught by him in class.

Unpublished Manuscript Sources

MS Diary of A.C. Benson in the Library at
Magdalene College, Cambridge (for published
extracts see Select Bibliography).

Scrapbook of Dr Cyril Alington in the possession of
Lady Home.

Letters to Lionel Smith in the possession of Edward
Hodgkin Esq.

Unpublished memoir of B.J.W. Hill *Eton Remembered
1937–75*.

MS Diary of Brian Howard for 1921 and Chapter 1
of Robert Byron's unfinished autobiography
Remember the Morning, both in the archives of the
School Library, Eton College.

Periodicals and Printed Collections

Eton College Chronicle.

Etoniana (Eton, 1904–75) ed. R.A. Austen Leigh and
others.

SELECT BIBLIOGRAPHY

This brief list includes the title and date of publication of most of the works cited in the text and notes and of some that are not so cited but have influenced the author's ideas or extended his knowledge of matters dealt with in this book. Two of the most suggestive and illuminating works that fall within the second category are P.S.H. Lawrence's *The Encouragement of Learning* (Wilton, 1980) and the same author's *An Eton Camera 1850–1919* (Wilton, 1980). The first is a selection from *Etoniana* (see preceding entry), the second a remarkably interesting collection of early photographs, both edited with much out-of-the-way knowledge aptly and entertainingly deployed.

Where no place of publication is given, London is to be understood.

Acton, Harold *Memoirs of an Aesthete* (1948)
Ainger, A.C. *Eton Sixty Years Ago* (1917)
Ayer, A.J. *Part of My Life* (1977)

Baring, Maurice *The Puppet Show of Memory* (1922)
Barlow, N. and Van Oss, O. *Eton Days* (1976)
Benson, A.C.*Fasti Etonenses* (Eton, 1899)
    The Diary of A.C. Benson, ed. Percy Lubbock (1926)
    Edwardian Excursions from the Diaries of A.C. Benson
    1898–1904 ed. David Newsome (1981)
    see also Newsome, David.
Birley, Robert *The History of College Library* (Eton, 1970)
    One Hundred Books in Eton College Library (Eton, 1970)
Bland, H.M. *Birds in an Eton Garden* (1935)
Byrne, L.S.R. and Churchill, E.L.
    Changing Eton (1937)

Churchill, E.L. see Byrne

Connolly, Cyril *Enemies of Promise* (1938, rev.ed. 1949)
   The Evening Colonnade (1973)
   A Romantic Friendship The Letters of Cyril Connolly to Noel
   Blakiston (1975)
Cory, William Johnson
   Ionica (1858, n.e. 1905)
   A Guide to Modern English History, i (1880)
   Letters and Journals (Oxford, 1897)

Esher, Reginald Brett, 2nd Viscount *Ionicus* (1923)
Fergusson, Bernard *Eton Portrait* (1937)
Fletcher, C.R.L. *Edmond Warre* (1922)

Green, Henry *Pack My Bag* (1940, n.e. 1979)

Harrod, Roy *John Maynard Keynes* (1951)
Heygate, John *Decent Fellows* (1930)
Hill, M.D. *Eton & Elsewhere* (1928)
Honey, J.R. de S. *Tom Brown's Universe: The Development of the
   Victorian Public School (1977)*
Howard, Brian (ed.) *The Eton Candle* (Eton, 1922)
Hussey, Christopher *Eton College* (4th edn. 1952)

James, M.R. *Eton and Kings* (1926)

Knox, R.A. *Patrick Shaw-Stewart* (1920)

Lubbock, Percy *Shades of Eton* (1929)
   see also Benson, A.C.
Luxmoore, H.E. *Letters of H.E. Luxmoore*
   ed. A.B. Ramsay (Cambridge, 1929)
   Noblesse Oblige (Eton, 1885)
Lyttelton, Edward *Memories and Hopes* (1925)

Mack, Edward C. *Public Schools and British Opinion 1780–1860* (1938)
   Public Schools and British Opinion since 1860 (New York, 1941)
Mackenzie, Faith Compton *William Cory: a biography* (1950)
Macnaghten, Hugh *Fifty Years of Eton* (1924)
Maxwell-Lyte, H.C. *A History of Eton College* (1440-1910) (4th edn.
   1911)

Newsome, David *On the Edge of Paradise: A.C. Benson The Diarist* (1980)
  Godliness and Good Learning (1961)

Pfaff, R.W. *Montague Rhodes James* (1980)
Powell, Anthony *To Keep the Ball Rolling*: The memoirs of Anthony Powell vol.i. *Infants of the Spring* (1976)

Rose, Kenneth *The Later Cecils* (1975)

Salt, H.S. *Memories of Bygone Eton* (1928)
Stansky, P. and Abrahams, W. *The Unknown Orwell* (1972)

Van Oss, *see* Barlow

Walton, Izaak *Sir Henry Wotton* (1651. I have used the reprint in Wordsworth *Eccles. Biog.* 2nd ed. 1818 vol v)
Wolffe, Bertram *Henry VI* (1981)
Wortham, H.E. *Victorian Eton and Cambridge being the Life and Times of Oscar Browning* (1927, n.e. 1956)

INDEX

Notes

1. Where utility has seemed to me to conflict with consistency I have preferred the former. Thus those who have progressed through a series of titles or have been rewarded as they entered life's harbour with the salute of a peerage will be found under the name by which they are best known. On the same principle I have not given a peer his full style unless there seemed some possibility of confusion.

2. I have given the date at which Head Masters and Provosts mentioned in the index entered on their tenure of these posts (so often held in succession). Where a man held only one of the two I have given the opening and closing dates.

of, 90–1
Leaving Portraits, 42
Leigh, Edward Austen, 103
Leslie, Sir Shane, 200
Ley, H.G., 193
Library, College, 30, 43
School,
    founded by Newborough, 35
Lubbock, Percy, on Warre, 73, 75
Luxmoore, H.E., 77–80, 152–3
    mentioned 58, 69, 85, 103, 127
Lyttelton, Alfred, 89
Lyttelton, Edward (Head Master
    1905–16), 76–7, 89–92, 94, 108,
    115
Lyttelton, G.W., 117–120, 123–4,
    167
    mentioned 69, 89, 143, 169

Macnaghten, Hugh, 88, 114ff, 127,
    200
Madan, Geoffrey, 90
Maitland, F.W., 69
Marsden, H.K., 106–7, 192–3
Marten, C.H.K. (Provost 1945–9),
    114–5, 153, 178, 180
Martineau, R.C., 166, 174 *note*, 196
Mary I, 27, 28
Master in College, 104, 192
Masters, 38, 143, 145–7, 151, 159,
    191
    recruitment of, 19
    criticised by Scotch private
    tutor, 44
    behaviour and quality in Keate's
    time, 46ff, 197; and in Hawtrey's
    58ff; and in Alington's 112–120,
    145–7, 191–3, pay 160–1
Mathematics, 87, 146
Military enthusiasm, of Cory and
    Warre 69–70, 73
    resistance to, 88
Mill, J.S., influence on Cory, 63
Modern Languages, 49, 51, 62, 87,
    113, 116
Money, 161ff

Montem, 55, 154
Mynors, Sir Roger, 110, 160, 180

Newborough, John (Head Master
    1690–1711), 35–6
Newcastle scholarship, 58
    its foundation, 52
New College, 13, 102
Newsome, David, 85, 86 *note*,
    quoted 124
Numbers, 37–8

Old Boy Network, 12
    historical origins of, 45, 182–4
Old Etonian Association, 91,
    183–4
Oppidan(s) (*see also* Glossary),
    19–20, 40, 72, 87, 110, 142–4,
    164, 181, 188–9
Orwell, George (Eric Blair), 11,
    78, 105, 110, 113, 120, 141–2,
    180
Oxford (*see also* under individual
    colleges), 13, 16, 25, 72, 175

Parker, Eric, 180
Parliament, O.E. members of, 182
Philistinism, 107–8, 144, 169
Plays, 27, 155
Political Society, The, 113, 160,
    179–80
Politics, consciousness of, 36,
    50–3, 160, 180–2
Pop *see* Eton Society
Powell, Anthony, 110, 132, 134,
    135, 141, 149
Praed, Winthrop Mackworth, 14,
    46, 195 *note*
Printing (at Eton), 30, 190

Quickswood, Lord, *see* Cecil, Lord
    Hugh

Rawlins, F.H., 103
Rebellion (School), 37
Reform, by parliament,